Unbuilt Oxford

Unbuilt Oxford

Howard Colvin

Yale University Press
New Haven and London 1983

K.V.T. et R.I.McK.
collegis

Frontispiece. Detail from Humphry Repton's proposed improvements to Magdalen College, 1801.

Designed by Stephanie Hallin.
Filmset in Monophoto Ehrhardt and printed in Great
Britain by Butler & Tanner Ltd, Frome, Somerset.

Library of Congress Cataloging in Publication Data

Colvin, Howard Montagu.
   Unbuilt Oxford.
   Bibliography: p.
   Includes index.
   1. University of Oxford—Buildings—Designs and plans
—History—Addresses, essays, lectures. 2. Hawksmoor,
Nicholas, 1661–1736. I. Title.
LF510.C64 1983   727'.3'0942574   83-42870
ISBN 0-300-03016-9

Contents

Preface

THE MIGHT-HAVE-BEENS of history are not popular with historians. Why something did not happen may be a proper subject for historical inquiry, but a hypothetical train of events is emphatically not.

For the architectural historian, however, the might-have-beens of his subject are in rather a different category. Buildings that failed to get erected are a perfectly legitimate subject of inquiry, for many of them exist on paper, and we can often evaluate them as well as we can existing buildings, not to mention destroyed ones. Moreover, unlike the military and political might-have-beens, the architectural ones often represent a genuine choice that offered itself at the time – a choice between rival architects, between different styles, between different interpretations of the same style. So by studying these rejected alternatives we can gain a better idea of the reasons that determined the final choice, and see more clearly the place of a given building in architectural history.

Oxford is a place in which we are exceptionally well placed to study this phenomenon, partly because college and university archives have been better kept than most, and partly because Oxford University consists of self-governing corporations of equals rather than of hierarchical institutions dominated by one man or woman. To build in Oxford means convincing twenty or thirty colleagues of the rightness of one's ideas, and many are the schemes that have failed to find favour with a Building Committee or Governing Body. For every Dr. Clarke or Warden Smith (to name two enthusiastic patrons of architecture in Oxford) there have been a score of sceptical fellows, worried about the cost, dubious about the design and characteristically reluctant to come to a decision. Oxford, as someone said, is a 'hotbed of cold feet'. Architecturally it is a graveyard of rejected designs, and it is to the resurrection of some of these abortive projects that the following pages are devoted.

Although this book is primarily about buildings that have never existed except in men's imaginations, or that have been built in a form substantially different from the one originally envisaged, it is also in some degree a series of case-studies in the academic patronage of architecture. By concentrating on the moments of choice I hope to illustrate that patronage at work, and to single out not only those periods when it has been most successful, but also those when it has failed. For failures there have been – some of nerve, some of judgement and some of finance. Architecture, like politics, is very much 'the art of the possible'. Dons may live in ivory towers, but they do not often build them. So in universities, as elsewhere, architecture is always a compromise between the visionary and the practicable. Sometimes, as in Nicholas Hawksmoor's scheme for a Romanised Oxford, or Austen Harrison's for a Siculo-Norman college, the visionary has so far exceeded the practicable as to fail almost completely of realisation. Sometimes, as in the Science Area, the practicable has won all too complete a victory over the visionary. Only very occasionally, as in the case of the Radcliffe Library, has the visionary rather than the practicable prevailed.

The practicable is there for all to see. But the evidence of the visionary is hidden from view in libraries and muniment rooms. (It is also tragically perishable: for every original drawing illustrated in these pages, twenty have been lost through carelessness or ignorance.) So if, in this book, it has been the visionary that has been emphasised at the expense of the practicable, it has been in order to redress the historical record, not to imply that the wrong decisions have often been made by those who, despite all their failings as corporate architectural patrons, have after all created what by common consent is one of the most remarkable concentrations of beautiful and interesting buildings in Europe.

*   *   *

The reader who expects to find in this book a comprehensive account of its subject will be disappointed. This is not a systematic study, but a series of essays on the theme of 'unbuilt Oxford', and it makes no claim to completeness. Even if that has been its objective, the very large number of unexecuted designs of relatively recent date that are known to exist would have presented a problem: for even to have listed them all would have seriously upset the chronological balance of this book. It should also be made clear that my concern has been with architecture rather than with town-planning: I have devoted some space to Hawksmoor's town-planning projects because they were associated with some of his grandest architectural designs. But I have written nothing about the road and town-planning schemes of the 1940s and 1950s, because the architecture that was envisaged by their authors was for the most part not fully developed, and such indications of it as were afforded at the time show buildings of a banality that does not encourage further investigation.*

Although virtually every unexecuted design that has been discussed in the text is represented by a drawing or a photograph, it has been impossible, for reasons

* An exception must, however, be made in favour of Raymond Erith's elegant neo-Georgian design for a bridge over the Cherwell, made in 1954 to show that if a Meadow Road was necessary then at least the bridge need not be ugly. The original highly-finished drawing is in the Diploma Collection of the Royal Academy. See L. Dale, 'A Bridge for Oxford', *Architecture & Building*, July 1954.

of cost, fully to illustrate all the buildings actually erected. Views of most of these are easily accessible in the many books about Oxford, and in deploying a necessarily limited number of illustrations it has seemed more important to concentrate on what was not built.

That this book is as well illustrated as it is is due to a generous grant from the British Academy. I am also very much indebted to the authors of the plans and perspective drawings, Paul Draper and Daphne Hart, both of whom have, in interpreting my directions, done much to give accuracy and verisimilitude to architectural concepts that are often imperfectly recorded and sometimes to a large extent conjectural.

Professor David Henderson, Mr. J. Lankester, Mr. Bernard Fagg and the Warden of Wadham were kind enough to recall for my benefit past events in which they participated. Sir Norman Chester read and criticised my account of the designing of Nuffield College.

Others to whom I am indebted for help or information in one form or another include Miss J. Allard of the University Museum, Mrs. L. Archer (for information about designs by her father, Raymond Erith), Mr. Trevor Aston, Dr. R.A. Beddard, Mr. David Brock, Dr. David Butler, Mr. George Carter, Mrs. Eric Collieu, Mr. David Dean, Mr. M.R. Dudley, Dr. Kenneth Garlick, Mr. John Harris, Miss Barbara Harvey, Dr. J.R.L. Highfield, Mr. R.G. Hill of Toronto, Miss Diane Kay, Mr. Timothy Mowl, Mr. Stephen Otto, Mr. Harry Pitt, Mr. W.F. Price, Professor Alistair Rowan, Mr. F.W.L. Scovil, Professor Quintin Skinner, Mr. John Sparrow, Mr. David Sturdy, Sir John Summerson, Mr. R. Walters of the Oxford Union Society's Library, Dr. David Watkin, Mrs. K. Watson and Mr. Laurence Whistler.

For access to documents or drawings I am grateful to many librarians and archivists, in particular to Miss Pauline Adams (Somerville College), Miss R. Campbell (St. Antony's College), Dr. Jeremy Catto (Oriel College), Mr. Malcolm Graham (Oxford City archives), Dr. Gerald Harriss (Magdalen College), Miss C. Kennedy (Nuffield College), Dr. J.F.A. Mason (Christ Church), Dr. Leslie Mitchell (University College), Miss L. Montgomery (Worcester College), Mrs. B. Parry-Jones (Magdalen College), Mr. E.V. Quinn (Balliol College), Mr. J.S.G. Simmons (All Souls College) and Mr. John Veale (papers of the late Sir Douglas Veale).

Permission to reproduce drawings, photographs or engravings in their archives or collections was kindly given by the Ashmolean Museum, the Bodleian Library, the British Architectural Library and Drawings Collection, London, the Irish Architectural Archive, Dublin, the National Monuments Record, London, the Surveyor to Oxford University, the Warden and Fellows of All Souls, the Master and Fellows of Balliol, the Principal and Fellows of Brasenose, the Dean and Chapter of Christ Church, the President and Fellows of Corpus, the President and Fellows of Magdalen, the Warden and Fellows of Merton, the Warden and Fellows of New College, the Warden and Fellows of Nuffield, the Provost and Fellows of Oriel, the Provost and Fellows of Queen's, the Warden and Fellows of

St. Antony's, the President and Fellows of St. John's, the President and Fellows of Trinity, the Master and Fellows of University College, the Provost and Fellows of Worcester, Lady Anne Cavendish-Bentinck and Messrs. Chamberlin, Powell and Bon. Mr. Peter Brigham, the Hon. Godfrey Samuel and Mr. Maxwell Fry were so good as to allow me to reproduce drawings of which they hold the copyright.

I

Gothic Uncertainties

OF MEDIEVAL OXFORD much survives, but more has perished. Of what has been lost there are some traces: archaeology has recovered the plans of the two great friars' churches which were once the landmarks of what is now the Westgate Shopping Centre and its satellite car-park. Parts of the city wall survive here and there in college gardens and the backyards of shops. Many long-demolished college buildings can still be studied in Loggan's elegant and accurate engravings. And on still winter evenings Great Tom can still be heard tolling for the students of Christ Church as once it tolled for the monks of Osney.

But of what never existed except in men's hopeful imaginings there is very little evidence. No document survives like the one in which King Henry VI laid down the plan of his Cambridge college for posterity, no drawing like the one, dating probably from the fifteenth century, that shows a bell-tower such as he must have envisaged. What evidence we have in Oxford is architectural or archaeological rather than graphic or documentary. In the Divinity School the effects of a change of mind in the year 1440 are still clearly apparent. In that year, partly for reasons of taste and partly for reasons of economy, the university authorities instructed their master-mason, Thomas Elkyn, to abandon what they called 'the superfluous elaboration' (*supervacuam curiositatem*) of the work so far executed, and to continue in a simpler style. When Henry VI had similar misgivings about the design of Eton College Chapel in 1448, directing his mason to desist from 'superfluity of too great curious works of entaille [carving] and busy moulding', he made a clean sweep of all that had so far been built. But at Oxford the university could not afford to undo work already cut and laid, and so beneath the simplified jambs of the 1440s the more elaborate mouldings of the 1430s remain in place as evidence of what was originally intended (fig. 2). By the time the vault was built in the

1. (*facing page*) The Divinity School as completed in the 1470s (Thomas Photos, Oxford).

2. The Divinity School, showing the jamb of a window with mouldings simplified in accordance with the University's instructions to its master mason in the year 1440 (Thomas Photos, Oxford).

1

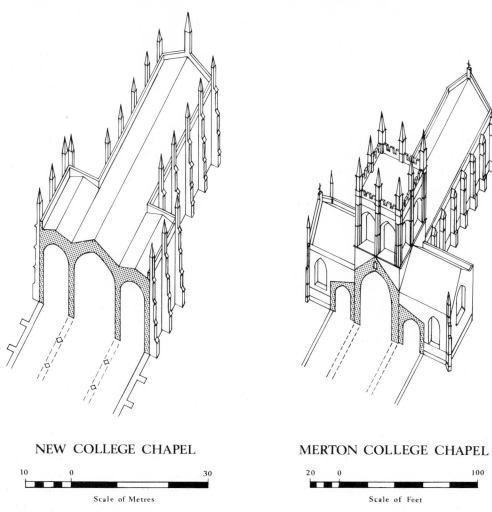

NEW COLLEGE CHAPEL

| 10 | 0 | | 30 |
Scale of Metres

MERTON COLLEGE CHAPEL

| 20 | 0 | | 100 |
Scale of Feet

3. The incomplete chapels of New College (*left*) and Merton (*right*), showing how the former has a truncated nave and no transepts and the latter transepts and no nave (drawn by Daphne Hart).

1470s the utmost elaboration was once again in fashion, so the completed building is a stratified monument to the pendulum of fifteenth-century taste (fig. 1).

The chapels of two medieval colleges show signs of incompleteness. Merton College chapel was obviously intended to be cruciform, but lacks its nave; New College, less obviously, has a chapel whose aisled nave is cut off after the second bay (fig. 3). At Merton the intention to build a nave is evident from the blocked-up archways and from the ghost of its roof against the west wall of the tower. At New College the site for a nave of normal length was not available when work on the college began in 1380, and by the time the property in question had been acquired by the Founder in 1388-9, it was evidently realised that a two-bay nave was quite sufficient for a college which (unlike Merton) had no parochial responsibilities. In fact the decision to truncate the chapel must have been made while building was still in progress. What had been begun as a nave ended as an ante-chapel, and the site of the missing bays was devoted to a cloister. But in the

Founder's statutes the ante-chapel is invariably referred to as a 'nave', and evidence of the change of mind can still be seen in some architectural details, notably the lack of any bonding between the north and south walls of the ante-chapel and the west wall. In the end Merton too found a nave superfluous and followed the example of New College. Such was the prestige of William of Wykeham's foundation as a model of collegiate planning that in the course of the next two-and-a-half centuries six other colleges did the same. The T-shaped chapel that resulted became in fact a characteristic peculiarity of Oxford college architecture. It even survived the Reformation, proving as acceptable to Anglican fellows as it had done to their Catholic predecessors. What originally must have accommodated extra altars for private masses now served as a dignified vestibule full of monuments and other ecclesiastical paraphernalia. In this form New College's truncated nave lived on at All Souls, Magdalen, Wadham, Oriel, Brasenose and formerly at Queen's (fig. 4).

If any other abortive plans were made for medieval Oxford colleges they have long been forgotten. It is idle to speculate about the architectural form that the still-born London College would have taken had it survived its founder Richard Clifford, Bishop of London (d. 1421), and we may pass over the curious problem presented by the unfinished Cistercian college of St. Bernard (now St. John's), whose disproportionately large kitchen gave promise of more food than could be consumed, even by the most gluttonous of monks, in its comparatively minute hall.

But in Wolsey's grand foundation of Cardinal College (1525) we are confronted with a major work of Tudor architecture cut short by its founder's fall in 1529 and left unfinished to the present day. No 'plott' or 'device' - the contemporary terms for plans and specifications - remains to tell us exactly how Cardinal College would have been completed had Wolsey's fall been delayed for another year or two. What we do know is that Wolsey's college was to have consisted of a cloistered quadrangle - the largest in Oxford - with the hall on the south side, the chapel on the north, an entrance-tower on the west, and further towers at the south-west and south-east corners. As soon as the chapel was finished the old priory church of St. Frideswide (now the cathedral) was to be demolished. The hall and the three principal ranges were built and the west end of the nave of the priory church had already been pulled down when Wolsey's fall put the whole future of his college in doubt. Eventually it was re-established as a royal foundation, but no money was forthcoming from Henry VIII for the building of the chapel or for the completion of the cloister, and for well over a hundred years Christ Church remained a three-sided quadrangle open to the north, where only the footings of Wolsey's chapel separated it from Blue Boar Lane. Only in the 1660s was the northern side of the quadrangle filled in by Dean Fell as a range of lodgings uniform with the others (fig. 5), while the upper part of Tom Tower was completed by Wren in a manner 'less busy' (as he put it) than the elaborately detailed lower stage designed by Wolsey's masons. We are so conditioned by the symmetrical front that resulted, balanced at each end by a low projecting bastion, that it is

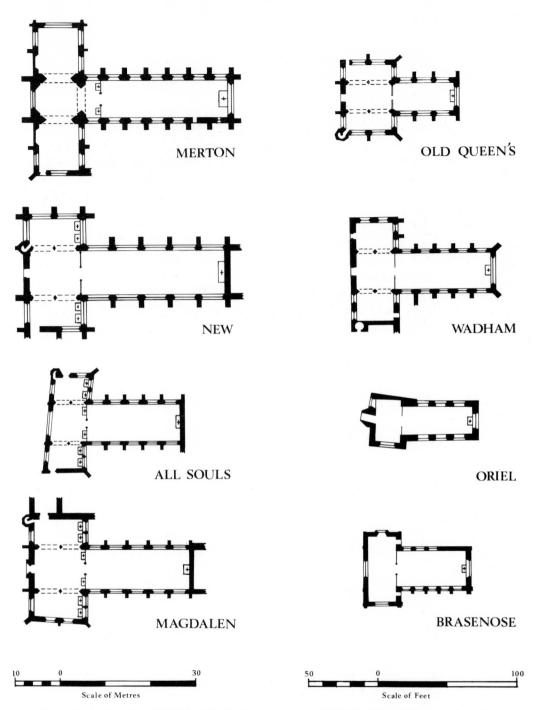

MERTON

OLD QUEEN'S

NEW

WADHAM

ALL SOULS

ORIEL

MAGDALEN

BRASENOSE

10   0   30

Scale of Metres

50   0   100

Scale of Feet

4. Oxford college chapels which follow the T-shaped plan established at New College at the end of the fourteenth century (drawn by Daphne Hart).

difficult to envisage the relatively irregular front that the Tudor masons had intended, with the mass of the chapel on the left only roughly balanced on the right by a tower whose lower stage still overlooks St. Aldate's. This tower was, so

4

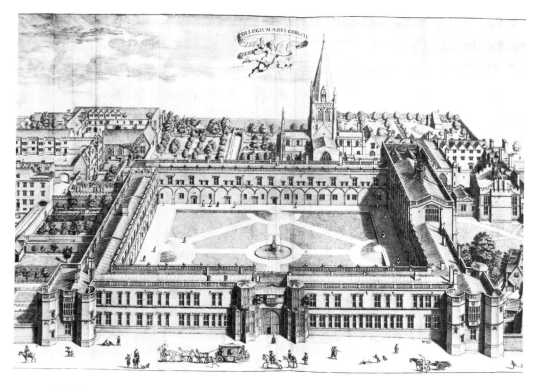

one of Wolsey's entourage reported in December 1526, already 'within four feet as high' as the adjoining lodgings. But it was never to rise above them, and although its general character can be deduced from its massive walls and polygonal corner turrets, the form of its intended upper stages must remain for ever conjectural. There is equal uncertainty about the tower which was to rise over the staircase at the east end of the hall. As for the chapel, its foundations were by the end of 1526 already 'equal with the ground' and in the course of 1528 the carpentry of its roof was being framed in the woods at Sonning in Berkshire. But although its plinth was still there to be seen and sketched by Aubrey in the seventeenth century (fig. 6), no one took the trouble to record the alignment or dimensions of the masonry before it was swept away by Fell to make way for his new range. The

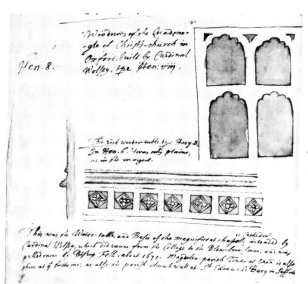

5. (*above*) Cardinal College: Loggan's engraving of 1675, showing on the left the range of lodgings built on the site of the chapel and in the centre Wolsey's entrance gateway, not yet completed by the addition of Tom Tower. Within the quadrangle the intended cloister has left its mark on the walls.

6. Cardinal College: John Aubrey's sketch showing the plinth which was all that was built of Wolsey's great chapel, drawn before it was destroyed in the reign of Charles II (Bodleian Library, MS. Top. gen. c.25, f.164).

7. Cardinal College: a conjectural drawing by Daphne Hart showing the principal features of the college as Wolsey envisaged it. There is architectural or documentary evidence for all the component buildings, but the form of the chapel is entirely conjectural, and so are the upper parts of the tower over the entrance gateway and of the towers at the south-west and south-east corners.

exact size and architectural character of Wolsey's great chapel are therefore matters for conjecture. One assumes that the proud cardinal would not have been content with anything much smaller in scale or less in magnificence than King's College Chapel in Cambridge, and it is King's Chapel that has formed the basis of Daphne Hart's drawing (fig. 7). Of one thing we can be certain: Cardinal College Chapel is the greatest and saddest of all the might-have-beens in Oxford's architectural history. Had Wolsey's fall been delayed just by one or two years, King's College Chapel – 'perhaps the greatest achievement of English architecture in any age', and certainly the supreme monument of English Gothic – would at least have had a rival in Oxford.

II

Retarded Renaissance

THE FIRST HALF of the seventeenth century was a period of intensive building activity in Oxford. Not only were the Schools Quadrangle and the two transverse ends added to Duke Humfrey's Library, but three new colleges were founded, two existing ones were entirely rebuilt and several others were much enlarged.

So far as the Bodleian Library is concerned, only a single drawing survives from a major building programme which began in 1610 with the construction of the eastern (or 'Arts') End of the Library and concluded in 1635 with that of the western (or 'Selden') End. It is only the roughest of sketch-plans, but it is the earliest surviving drawing for an Oxford building (executed or otherwise) that is still in existence (fig. 8). What it represents is an 'Arts End' of about the same breadth as the one actually built, but of little more than half its length from north to south, and lighted not (as now) by one large window in each end wall, but by three small ones. Rows of bookcases similar to those now in Duke Humfrey's Library run from north to south, those at each end being placed against the wall-space left between the small windows. This was the traditional arrangement of bookcases in sixteenth-century libraries, but on the continent (notably in the library at the Escorial, built by Philip II of Spain in 1584) free-standing bookcases had been abandoned in favour of wall-shelving, and this of course was the arrangement that was eventually adopted (for the first time in an English library)

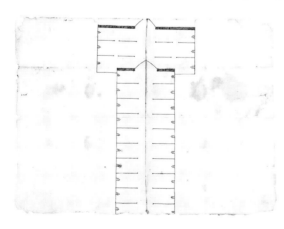

8. Bodleian Library: a sketch made in 1610 to show an arrangement of book-cases in the Arts End (*at top of drawing*) similar to that in Duke Humfrey's Library (*below*) (Bodleian Library, MS. Wood F.27, ff. 41ᵛ–42).

in the 'Arts End'. With the aid of galleries it enabled many more books to be housed in the space available, and satisfied Sir Thomas Bodley's expressed wish 'to cast our plottes in suche sort, as the uttermost advantage of roome may be taken'. It is one of these 'plottes' that survives to illustrate a moment of change in English library design.

In the colleges the building activity of the early seventeenth century reflected their growing importance as educational establishments. The medieval colleges had been small, exclusive, corporations of scholars with little responsibility for the mass of undergraduates who lived in the many academic halls that were scattered about the town. But by the end of the sixteenth century the colleges had taken over responsibility for housing and teaching the undergraduates, and the new buildings were designed to provide the necessary accommodation.

In a university whose religious observances had been transformed by the Reformation and whose intellectual attitudes were slowly responding to the Renaissance, all this new building activity might have been expected to produce a new type of college, classical in style and recognisably Anglican in its provision for religious worship. But this is not what happened. The first two post-Reformation foundations – Trinity and St. John's – both took over existing buildings, which they adapted to their purposes with relatively little alteration. The next two – Jesus and Wadham – remained faithful to the established traditions of Oxford collegiate architecture, and so did Oriel and University College when they were completely rebuilt in the second and third decades of the seventeenth century. At Oriel, Wadham and University College the layout was still essentially that established by William of Wykeham in the fourteenth century. Hall and chapel continued to be built end to end (or side by side) on one side of the quadrangle, and at Oriel, Wadham and Brasenose considerable ingenuity was exercised to accommodate a traditional T-shaped chapel. Though a new interest in symmetry can be detected (at Oriel, Wadham and University College the hall-and-chapel unit has been moved to the side facing the entrance in order to give axial formality to the quadrangle) the style of the doorways and fenestration remains for the most part obstinately Gothic. For domestic rooms flat-headed windows of sub-Gothic form were normal, while for halls and chapels 'the old fashion of church windows' – one, that is, with a pointed head and proper tracery – continued to find favour in Oxford as it did in Cambridge. If the voice of Tudor humanism was heard in the Schools, its visual expression was conspicuously absent from their walls. Few if any of the Italian craftsmen whom Wolsey patronised at Hampton Court were employed at Cardinal College, and even in the reign of Charles I Archbishop Laud preferred to adorn his own college of St. John the Baptist with a mannerist mixture of Gothic and classic rather than procure a pure Palladian design from the Surveyor of the King's Works. Elsewhere – at Wadham and Merton and most conspicuously in the Schools Quadrangle – a gauche assemblage of superimposed orders was the nearest that Jacobean Oxford ever got to embracing the principles of classical architecture.

In seventeenth-century Oxford architecture was in fact the most conservative of the visual arts. Only in sculpture and glass-painting was the university at all abreast with current fashion. Not a single building by Inigo Jones or his pupil John Webb was to be found in Oxford.

How are we to explain this state of affairs? Why was one of the intellectual centres of England not also a centre of architectural thought? The answer is that in Oxford art and intellect, if not actually estranged, were hardly on terms of intimacy. This was, of course, a situation of long standing, born of the medieval distinction between liberal and mechanical arts. Architecture, as a mechanical art, did not form part of the academic curriculum. Not a single architectural work is to be found in the surviving book-lists of Oxford academics between 1550 and 1650, and although a few copies of treatises such as Serlio and Vitruvius - the textbooks of Renaissance architecture - were available in Oxford libraries, they can have been little read. Thus men who habitually wrote and even spoke in Latin felt as yet no compulsion to give architectural expression to what for them was almost entirely a literary culture. Although Sir Henry Savile (Warden of Merton 1585-1621) was so experienced in building affairs that Sir Thomas Bodley regarded his opinion 'as the judgement of a mason', his understanding of classical architecture was manifestly limited. No Oxford don of his generation was as well informed in architectural matters as John Caius (1510-73), the founder of the Cambridge college which bears his name. There the gates of Humility, Virtue and Honour give architectural form to a concept that is characteristically humanist: the idea of Honour as the reward of *Virtus*, that is (in an academic context) of intellectual excellence. The three gates that Caius built to symbolise this progression from initial humility to ultimate honour represent a serious attempt to use appropriate classical forms derived in part from Serlio, and the open-ended court with the Gate of Honour at its entrance is (for England) a precocious piece of Renaissance planning. But Caius - unique in Cambridge - had no counterpart in Oxford, where architecture was left largely to the masons, who continued to build in a version of the Gothic style with which they were familiar. Only in the gateway to the Physic Garden (1632) was something consistently classical attempted, though in Inigo Jones's estimation those who designed it did so but 'lamely'.

Nevertheless there must have been a few dons - and even some masons - who were dimly aware that architecturally speaking Oxford in the reign of Charles I was a Gothic backwater and who regretted that it should be so. What voices were raised in Hall or Common Room in favour of classical architecture we do not know, but one drawing exists to show that at University College an alternative scheme was considered which, had it been carried out, would have been as revolutionary in Caroline Oxford as Caius' gateways had been in Elizabethan Cambridge. With it there has miraculously survived a model of the traditional Gothic design that was (with a few modifications) begun in 1634 and eventually completed in the reign of Charles II (fig. 9). This model (fig. 10), consisting of elevational drawings stuck onto pasteboard and sewn together with thread at the corners, is the earliest example of its kind to have survived in England. Although the design it exhibits is Gothic, the idea of presenting it in model form derives

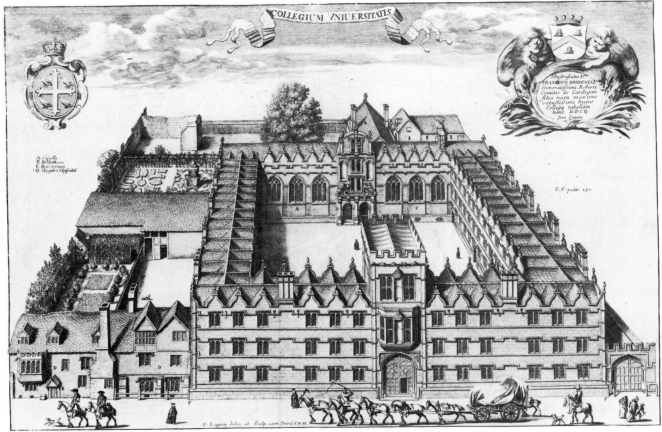

9. University College as rebuilt between 1634 and 1666, from Loggan's *Oxonia Illustrata* (1675).

ultimately from Renaissance Italy rather than from medieval Britain. All the Renaissance theorists, from Alberti onwards, emphasise the value of a model in enabling a design to be clearly comprehended in all its parts, and in England his advice had been echoed by Sir Henry Wotton in his *Elements of Architecture*, published in 1624. When the Canterbury Quadrangle was building at St. John's in 1631–6, £3 had been spent on having a wooden model of the building made by a joiner, and several pasteboard models are known to have been made in connection with the westward extension of the Bodleian Library in the 1630s. It was, therefore, with the best visual aids that the fellows of University College considered the merits of the Gothic design that was put before them (we do not know by whom) in or shortly before 1634.

Of the rival classical design (whose authorship is equally unknown) there is, unfortunately, no model, nor any elevation, but only the ground plan (fig. 11). What this shows is a quadrangle one hundred feet square (roughly the size of the quadrangle as built). On the street front the entrance is marked externally by a gateway which is flanked by columns or pilasters probably arranged in the manner of a simplified triumphal arch, inside by a columned vestibule. Opposite and on either side of the quadrangle there are porticos, marking the hall, the chapel and a building which would probably have housed the library on the upper floor. In

10

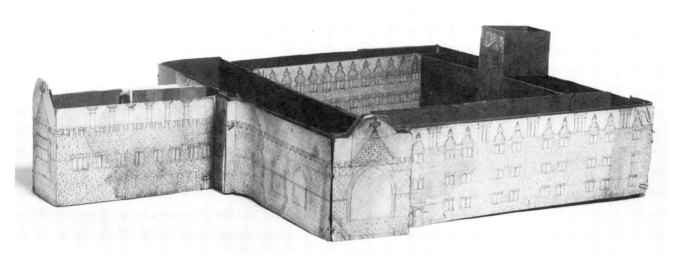

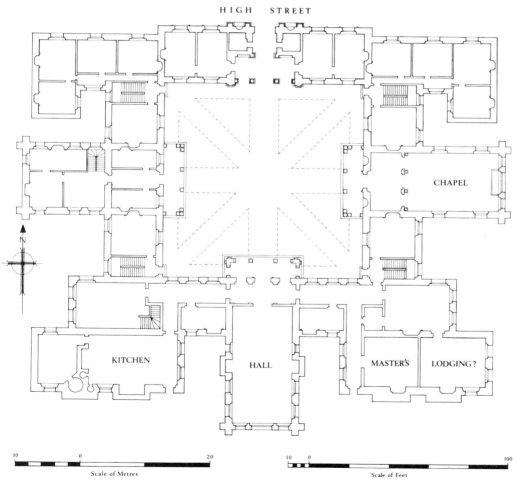

CHAPEL

KITCHEN

HALL

MASTER'S

LODGING?

Scale of Metres

Scale of Feet

10. University College: a pasteboard model made in or shortly before 1634. The buildings represented are, from left to right, the library, the chapel and the quadrangle. The college was built substantially in accordance with this design (University College archives).

11. University College: a plan made in or shortly before 1634, showing a college planned on classical principles, with three porticos in the quadrangle (redrawn from the original in University College archives).

11

between there are rooms, arranged on the familiar staircase principle. The façade to the street is symmetrical and the windows on either side of the gateway are emphasised by classical architraves, but the other external elevations are irregular and, although the quadrangle makes a fine show, the plan as a whole is awkward and uneconomical both of space and of building materials. The amount of living accommodation provided is, moreover, relatively small, and it is not surprising that the plan is endorsed: 'refused as inconvenient'. It is precious, nevertheless, as by far the earliest known design for an Oxford or Cambridge college that is consistently classical in style, and its very awkwardness shows how difficult it was to produce an acceptable alternative to the traditional plan that had served Oxford so well for the last two and a half centuries.

III

The Limits of a Private Purse

THE BUILDING which effectively introduced classical architecture to Oxford was the Sheldonian Theatre, built in 1664–9 as a place of assembly for the University and paid for by Gilbert Sheldon, Archbishop of Canterbury. The architect was Christopher Wren, then a young man of thirty-one. He held the Professorship of Astronomy at Oxford, but was already interesting himself in architectural matters, though as yet he had had little practical experience of building. For the architectural form Wren went direct to the monuments of ancient Rome. Latin was the language of learning, and when an academic turned architect it was natural that he should look to classical antiquity for his architectural vocabulary. The type of Roman building that seemed best adapted to the purpose was the theatre, for theatres were designed for the performance of ceremonies in the presence of a large, seated, audience. Plans and elevations of Roman theatres were known to Wren from architectural text-books such as those of Vitruvius and Serlio, and gave him the idea of a D-shaped building with tiered seats inside and an exterior dignified by columns and arches.*

But the needs of ancient Rome and those of seventeenth-century Oxford were not identical. The Roman theatre was an open arena, protected from the elements only by awnings, whereas an English one required the permanent shelter of a roof. To introduce load-bearing columns would ruin the resemblance to an ancient theatre, so Wren had to cover his seventy-foot span without them. No timbers of sufficient length were, of course, available, so Wren designed a trussed roof, made up of scarfed and jointed timbers, which covered the required space without any intermediate support. This feat gained him great credit in scientific and architectural circles, and made the roof of the Sheldonian Theatre a landmark in roof construction. From below all this technical ingenuity was, however, concealed from view by the flat expanse of the ceiling, painted in such a way as to maintain

* The idea of an academic assembly hall in the form of a theatre was not entirely novel, for the University of Naples had built one some sixty years earlier, and engravings of it had been published (G. Barrionuevo, *Panegyricus . . .*, Naples, 1616). But the Neapolitan theatre, though semicircular in plan, with tiered seats and galleries, was part of a larger building, within which it formed an apse or exedra. Even if Wren knew of it, which is by no means certain, it could not have provided him with any guidance in designing a free-standing building.

12. The Sheldonian Theatre in use in the eighteenth century. The Vice-Chancellor sits in the middle of the curved auditorium, with the audience partly behind and partly in front of him (from a drawing dated 1781 by S. H. Grimm in the British Museum, Department of Manuscripts).

13. Design for a theatre by Inigo Jones, showing the semi-circular seating and the classical *scaenae frons* in front of which the actors performed (Worcester College Library I, 7 B and C).

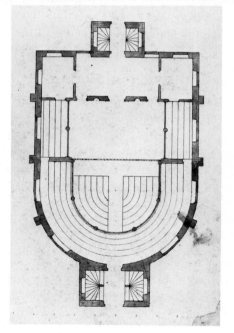

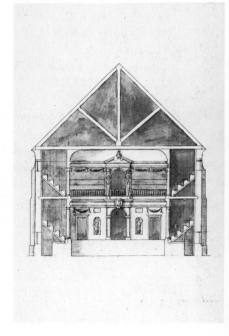

14

the illusion of a Roman theatre open to the sky. In planning the interior, Wren made another deviation from his Roman original. There is no stage against the flat southern wall, and the focus of attention is the Vice-Chancellor's chair in the middle of the semi-circular tiers of seating (fig. 12). Thus the functions of auditorium and stage are reversed, something that would have seemed odd to anyone familiar with the illustrations of Roman theatres in the architectural textbooks.

But there is reason to think that the Sheldonian Theatre as it was built did not fully realise Wren's intentions. According to *Parentalia*, the family history written by his son, 'This Theatre . . . [would have] been executed in a greater and better Style, with a view to the ancient Roman Grandeur discernible in the Theatre of

14. The Sheldonian Theatre: a conjectural drawing by Paul Draper showing the interior with provision for theatrical performances, including a *scaenae frons* of the sort Wren might have designed.

15. The Sheldonian Theatre: the exterior as built (D. Loggan, *Oxonia Illustrata*, 1675).

16. The Sheldonian Theatre: a conjectural drawing by Paul Draper showing the exterior with an Ionic order. There is reason to think that it was in some such form that Wren originally conceived the building. But no drawings exist so all the architectural details shown here are conjectural.

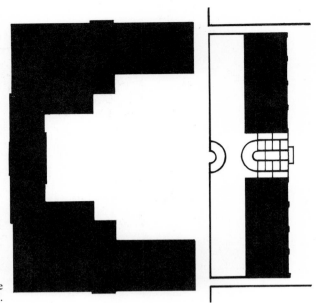

17. Winchester Palace: a block plan of the palace begun to Wren's designs in 1683.

Marcellus at Rome; but that he was obliged to put a stop to the bolder Strokes of his Pencil, and confine the Expence within the limits of a private Purse.'

In what way did Wren's original design differ from the executed building? Unfortunately none of his drawings for the Theatre have survived, but in 1663 he had a model made which he showed to the Royal Society. Two of those who saw the model, Henry Oldenburg and Abraham Hill, noted that the Theatre was to be used for performing plays, as well as for conferring degrees, etc., and Hill added that it was to be 'more exactly accommodated to the Roman architecture, than any now extant'. Now the existing building, though undoubtedly classical, hardly realises these expectations of Roman grandeur in its exterior, while its interior lacks the *scaenae frons* and back-stage areas necessary for theatrical performances. In fact it has rarely, if ever, been used as a playhouse. If we compare its plan with a design for a theatre made by Inigo Jones (fig. 13) and very likely to be identified with the Phoenix (or Cockpit) Theatre in Drury Lane built in 1616 and demolished in 1649, we can see what was lacking in the way of theatrical accommodation. We can also wonder whether this short-lived London theatre, which Wren might have seen when he was a schoolboy at Westminster, could to some extent have provided him with a prototype for his Oxford building. Like the Sheldonian, it was in principle a much simplified version of an antique theatre, complete with *scaenae frons*. Externally there was no Roman grandeur about the Cockpit Theatre, and if Wren hoped (as his son believed) to emulate the Theatre of Marcellus, he must have intended to dignify the exterior by a classical order not merely on the flat southern elevation facing the Divinity School, but on the curved northern portion as well. In fact what we have is a podium of channelled masonry such as might serve as the base for such an order, immediately surmounted by a row of

18

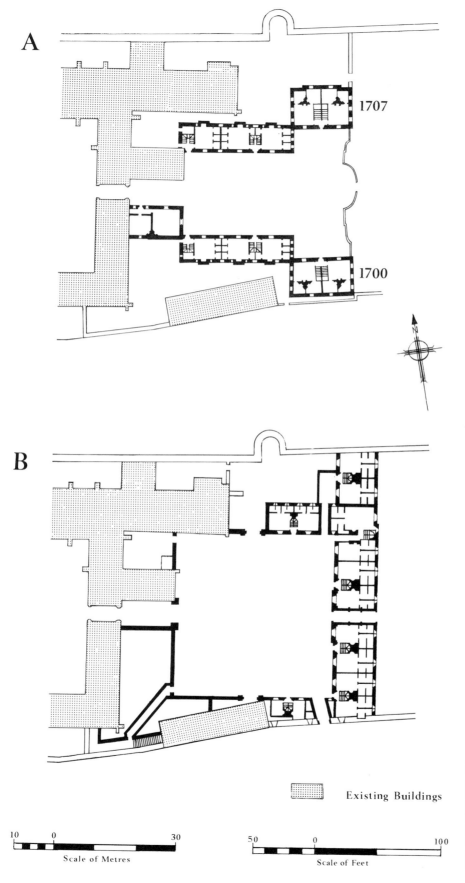

A

1707

1700

N

B

Existing Buildings

18. New College: A. plan of the Garden Quadrangle with stepped-back wings, as designed by William Byrd in 1682 and built in stages between 1682 and 1707. B. alternative design by William Byrd for a closed quadrangle, made in 1682, as shown on an engraved plan in New College archives (drawn by Daphne Hart).

10   0   30
Scale of Metres

50   0   100
Scale of Feet

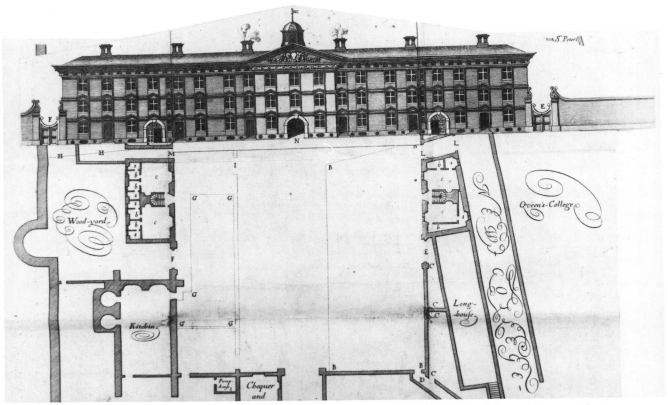

19. New College: one of William Byrd's proposals for the interior elevations of the closed quadrangle, corresponding to the plan shown in figure 18 (New College archives). The elevation is drawn on a hinged flap and the four bays at each end fold back at right angles to fit the plan.

windows suitable for an attic. The order of columns or pilasters which should intervene is missing (fig. 15). The result, as Sir John Summerson has wittily observed, 'is rather like a man with his trousers pulled up to his chin and his hat pulled over his nose'.

It may therefore be surmised that the features which 'the limits of a private purse' (that is, of Sheldon's benefaction) obliged Wren to omit were externally the order and internally the *scaenae frons*. The one would have given the Sheldonian Theatre the architectural consequence that it lacks when seen from Broad Street, the other would have made better sense of seating arrangements which in their existing form are designed for an audience facing a non-existent stage. Paul Draper's drawings, though entirely conjectural, show the kind of building that we may suppose was represented in Wren's original model (figs. 14, 16).

Simultaneously, Wren was engaged in designing a new residential block at Trinity, intended to house gentlemen commoners. There was much debate about the siting of this building, for which three alternative locations were contemplated, one to the south of the old quadrangle, 'towards Balliol', one in the Fellows' Garden to the north, and a third (favoured by Wren) in the adjoining Grove or

20

20. New College: the completed Garden Quadrangle, from a drawing attributed to Michael Burghers (Ashmolean Museum).

21. Trinity College: design for adding stepped-back wings to the Garden Quadrangle, as illustrated in the *University Almanack* for 1756, but first proposed soon after 1730 (Ashmolean Museum).

College Garden. An estimate by Wren for the southern site survives, together with a curiously amateurish plan for a square block with an oval staircase projecting in the middle of one front. Eventually the Fellows' Garden was fixed on as the site of a new three-sided quadrangle, open on the east to the College Garden. The north side was built in 1665-8, the west in 1682. Each consisted of a neat pedimented block containing two staircases, a type which Wren was to repeat in the Williamson Building at Queen's in 1671-4. These were buildings of no great pretensions, but they were important as precedents for a collegiate architecture based on classical conventions. They showed that there was an alternative to mullioned windows and mannerist gables and as the beginning of an open-ended court the Trinity block was the first in Oxford to break through the closed medieval quadrangle. The second was the Garden Quadrangle at New College, built in stages from 1682 to 1707 (fig. 18).

The Garden Quadrangle was not designed by Wren, but by an Oxford master-mason named William Byrd. Byrd was well known to Wren, having in 1666-9 been responsible for the stone-carving at the Sheldonian Theatre (including the fourteen bearded terms better, though erroneously, known as 'the Emperors' Heads'). In 1683, moreover, he contracted to erect the south wing of Charles II's new palace at Winchester to Wren's designs. Now in planning Winchester Palace Wren had Le Vau's Versailles in mind: he stepped back the wings to give added consequence to the central portico and provide a wide view over the town from the royal apartments (fig. 17). Byrd, on the other hand, started with the idea of adding a further closed quadrangle to New College, and his proposal is illustrated by an engraved plan with hinged pasteboard elevation still preserved in the college archives (fig. 19). Although the commencement of work on the quadrangle actually preceded Byrd's employment at Winchester, it looks very much as if it was a preview or foreknowledge of Wren's design for the palace that led to the change of plan at New College. The inner wings were built by Byrd in 1682-4, the outer ones being added to a corresponding design in 1700-7 (fig. 20). Early in the 1730s the fellows of Trinity, having rebuilt the north range of the Durham Quadrangle to match Wren's new block opposite, thought of following the example of New College by adding stepped-back wings to their Garden Quadrangle. The design was illustrated in the University Almanack for 1732. Nothing came of it, but its repetition in the Almanack for 1756 (fig. 21) suggests that the idea was kept alive throughout the reign of George II.

IV

Dr. Clarke's Portfolios

WREN'S TRIUMPH over 'the Gothic rage' (*rabies Gothorum*) was celebrated in Latin verse by Corbett Owen, a student of Christ Church, who composed a 'Pindaric ode' on the Sheldonian Theatre and its architect. But by 1669 Wren had left Oxford to become Surveyor of the King's Works, and the University might once more have lost the architectural initiative but for the efforts of two talented amateurs: Dean Aldrich of Christ Church (d. 1710) and Dr. George Clarke of All Souls (d. 1736). For nearly fifty years no major building was undertaken in Oxford without their advice, and it was due largely to their interest and enthusiasm that in Georgian Oxford the conscious patronage of architecture became a prominent feature of university life. For Aldrich architecture was only one of many accomplishments. His writings included editions of Greek and Latin texts, a work on geometry and a well-known textbook on logic as well as a systematic treatise (never completed) on architecture. Based largely on Vitruvius and Palladio, this was a theoretical rather than a practical work, but Aldrich was more than just an academic student of architecture. He was in fact an accomplished draughtsman and from 1676 until his death most of the University Almanacks were engraved to designs either made or prescribed by him. He was the first Oxford don since Wren to take a serious interest in architecture and his status, first as head of a house and then as Vice-Chancellor, made him more influential than a mere professor. Tragically, he directed that all his papers should be destroyed after his death, so very little survives in the way of sketches or unexecuted designs to supplement the bare record of his architectural achievement, which comprises only two or three buildings: the Peckwater Quadrangle at Christ Church, All Saints Church and (probably) the Fellows' Building at Corpus.

Peckwater (1706-14) consists of three ranges of rooms, forming three sides of a large quadrangle. For the first time in Oxford collegiate architecture each elevation is unified by an order (Ionic). The juxtaposition of three identical façades is a little awkward, but the effect of the whole is grandly classical, and at a time when Vanbrughian baroque was in the ascendant elsewhere, Peckwater is remarkable as the affirmation of an academic classical style that is almost Palladian in character. The fourth side could not be closed without impeding access to Merton Street, and here Aldrich planned an insulated building distinguished from the remainder of the quadrangle by a monumental Corinthian order. It has often been supposed that this was intended to house a library, but the engraved plans (fig. 22) clearly show sets of rooms on the ground floor and staircases which promise more such rooms on the upper floors. In the event this fourth range of rooms – one of the most magnificent ever planned in Oxford – was never built, and its place was taken by Dr. Clarke's library.

Outside his own college Aldrich appears to have had few opportunities to practise architecture. In fact All Saints Church (1701-10) is the only other building for which his authorship is well established. It was on 8 March 1699/1700 that the spire of the medieval church collapsed, so injuring in its fall the rest of the structure that total rebuilding was deemed to be necessary. An appeal for £4,800 was launched, and a body of trustees was appointed to administer the money subscribed. One of them was the Dean of Christ Church, Aldrich himself; the others were the Vice-Chancellor and Mayor for the time being, the Provost of Queen's, the Rector of Lincoln, Thomas Rowney, Esq., M.P., and the Recorder. Later they were joined by the Master of University College, Dr. Charlett. No record of their deliberations has been preserved, but one of their first decisions must have been to settle the design upon which the church was to be rebuilt, and to have it engraved by Sturt for circulation to 'the Nobility, Gentry and Clergy and to all other Pious and well disposed Persons'. Later on a smaller version of the engraving was commissioned from Michael Burghers and distributed in the same way. The drawing from which Sturt's engraving was made was formerly at Welbeck Abbey and is now in the R.I.B.A. Drawings Collection (fig. 23). Unfortunately, the name of the architect appears neither on the drawing nor on the engraving. But there is every reason to suppose that the design was due to Aldrich. Peshall, in his *History of Oxford*, published in 1773, states definitely that Aldrich 'designed the present most elegant and noble structure', and although his testimony is not quite contemporary, he is unlikely to have been mistaken in his information. As a trustee, Aldrich was bound to be consulted, and it was only natural that his colleagues should have turned to him for the design.

The church which the trustees proposed to build was strictly suited to the Church of England services of the eighteenth century, being simply a rectangle without any suggestion of a chancel. The rectangle was, it is true, arranged with its longer axis from east to west, but this orientation was almost nullified by the unbroken range of windows on all four sides except the west, and by the placing of the doorways in the middle of the north and south walls. The exterior was to be dignified by a Corinthian order of pilasters, and this order was to be reflected in the interior. The engraved plan shows that Aldrich originally proposed to arrange the internal pilasters in pairs in exactly the same way as the external ones, but in execution compound fluted pilasters were used in the interior instead of plain ones in pairs, and in this way the uncomfortable sensation that the church had been turned outside in was avoided. It is natural to compare Aldrich's Oxford church with the London City churches designed thirty years earlier by Wren. All Saints may, indeed, be regarded as an academic version of a Wren church of the

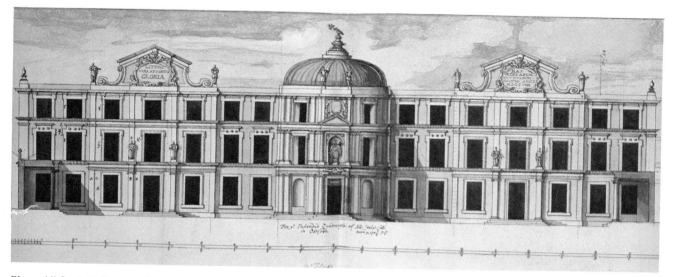

Pl. 1. All Souls College: design for a new building in Italian baroque style by John Talman, 1708 (Worcester College Library, no. 36).

Pl. 2. All Souls College: John Talman's design for a new hall in Italianate Gothic style, *c.* 1708. The central feature is a 'gilt brass' statue of the Founder (Archbishop Chichele), seated in a niche, and flanked on either side by statues of four ecclesiastics, one a 'Romish bishop', the second a 'Reformed Bishop', the third a clergyman in surplice and Geneva cap, and the fourth a Doctor of Divinity. One of each of these is seen here standing between the windows. Below, at ground level, 'statutes in brass of benefactors' are indicated. The pinnacles were to be gilded, and the finials or 'acroteres' (marked E) were to be 'of hard metal or brass gilded'. The east bay of the existing chapel is seen to the right, with a new parapet, etc., to match the hall (Worcester College Library, no. 41).

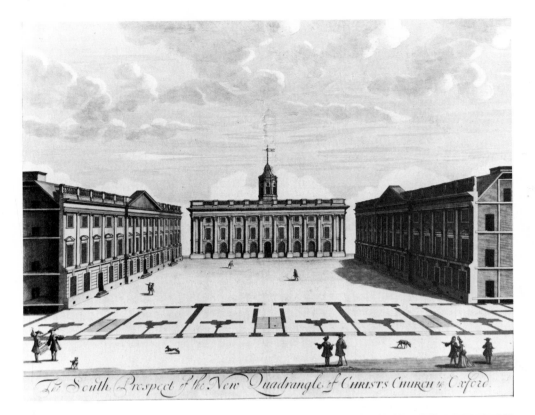

The South Prospect of the New Quadrangle of Christs Church in Oxford.

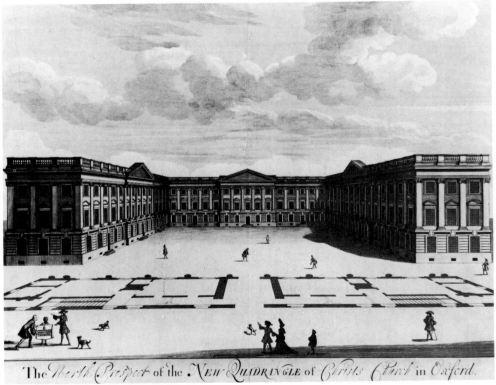

The North Prospect of the New Quadrangle of Christs Church in Oxford.

22. Christ Church: engravings showing the building intended by Dean Aldrich to close the south side of the Peckwater Quadrangle. The plan (*below*) clearly shows its residential character, with four sets of rooms on the ground floor and two staircases leading to further rooms above. Its place was taken by the library designed by Dr. George Clarke (fig. 53).

simpler type, 'corrected' by the rigid application of an order in order to comply with Aldrich's more strictly classical ideas.

It is, however, in his design for the proposed steeple that Aldrich's debt to Wren is most clearly apparent. For it is (as Sir John Summerson long ago pointed out) a much simplified version of Bow steeple. Had it been built in London there would have been no difficulty in accepting it as one of the later Wren steeples. But the engraved design was not to be carried out without several modifications. The altered treatment of the internal pilasters was one. Another was the placing of the entrances at the west ends of the lateral walls instead of in the middle, and the duplication of the portico on the north side, where it could be seen from the Turl. Most important of all were the alterations in the design of the steeple, for in the existing building the drum of the lantern has been heightened, the broken entablature of Aldrich's design had been replaced by a continuous architrave, frieze and cornice, the design of the balustrade has been changed, and the spire is no longer pierced by four circular openings in each facet.

How did Aldrich's original design come to be thus altered? So far as the body of the church is concerned, we do not know. It may be that Aldrich himself had second thoughts, as architects (especially amateur ones) often do. But the parish records make it clear that he was not responsible for the final design of the steeple. The body of the church, including the tower, was built between 1706 and 1709, when the churchwardens paid Mr. Frogley the joiner £17 9s. od. 'towards seating the church'. The interior must have been fitted up for worship by 1711, when £1 16s. od. was spent on re-erecting the seventeenth-century effigy of Alderman Levinz. Then the money ran out, and nothing more was done until 1718, when the Vestry Minutes record that Messrs. Townesend and Peisley, the contracting masons, were prepared 'to go on and finish the steeple' if the parish would guarantee to pay them £50 within the next two years. The parishioners agreed, and by 1720 the steeple was completed as we know it today (fig. 25).

Meanwhile Aldrich had died in 1710, and the parishioners had evidently consulted Nicholas Hawksmoor, who was by now much involved in other building schemes in Oxford (see Chapter V). There is no mention of Hawksmoor (or, indeed, of any other architect) in the parish records, but it is clear that he was consulted, for in the Bodleian Library there is a design by him for completing the steeple (fig. 24). Unfortunately the date has been torn away, but there can be little doubt that the drawing belongs to the period between the completion of the church in about 1710 and the decision to finish the steeple in 1718. It is a characteristic example of Hawksmoor's draughtsmanship, and represents a variation on the dome and peristyle theme which he was later to use in his designs for the Radcliffe Library and the Castle Howard Mausoleum.

Hawksmoor's design was not adopted: evidently the parishioners were not willing to depart so radically from the steeple with whose silhouette they had for so long been familiar from Sturt's and Burghers' engravings. Instead, a compromise design was worked out, incorporating features from both Aldrich and Hawksmoor. The drum was heightened and pierced by two rows of openings

23. All Saints Church: elevation of the original design attributed to Dean Aldrich, showing a central portico and a different design for the steeple (R.I.B.A. Drawings Collection, Cavendish-Bentinck loan).

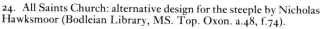

24. All Saints Church: alternative design for the steeple by Nicholas Hawksmoor (Bodleian Library, MS. Top. Oxon. a.48, f.74).

25. All Saints Church: the steeple as completed in 1720.

instead of one: the breaks were taken out of the entablature to give it the firm outline shown in Hawksmoor's sketch; an openwork parapet of a type much favoured by Hawksmoor was substituted for the conventional balustrading proposed by Aldrich: and the spire was deprived of its circular openings. The result was a bolder and a stronger design than the rather finicky one envisaged by Aldrich, which might not have stood out so well as an urban landmark. But both rejected designs have their merits, and their survival enables the student of unbuilt Oxford to enjoy two different variations on the same architectural theme, as well as the one that still graces the High Street today.

Aldrich's role as an architectural adviser is illustrated by two other buildings for which preliminary designs were circulated in engraved form, no doubt with the same object of attracting donations. The first is Trinity College Chapel, built in 1691–4 (fig. 28). Here two engravings show the progressive refinement of the design (figs. 26, 27). All that is definitely known is that Aldrich was one of the 'able judges in architecture' whose advice the College took before deciding to rebuild 'wholly upon new foundations'. Wren was also consulted, though too late to make any radical alteration to the design, the responsibility for which remains undetermined. The crudity of some features of the first version (especially the

29

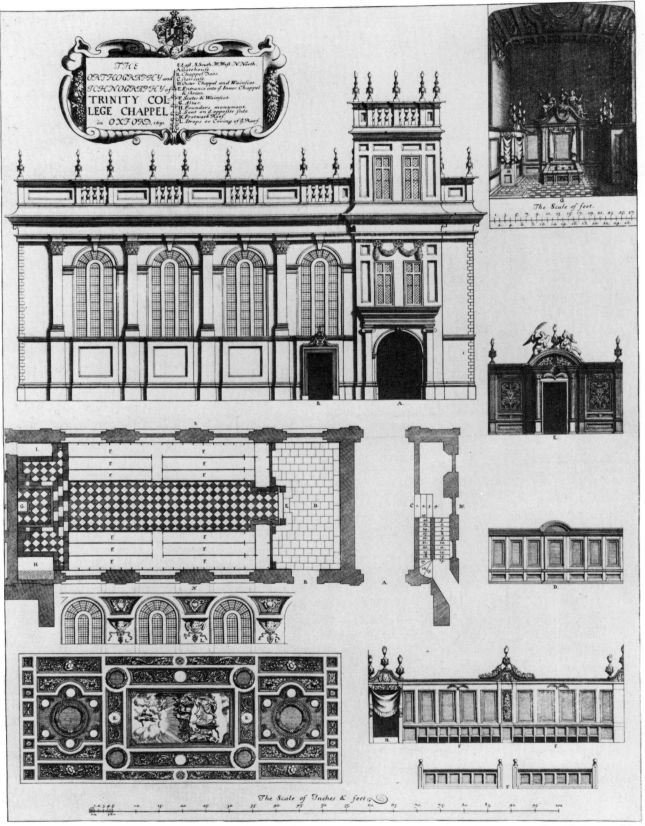

26, 27. Trinity College Chapel: two engravings by Michael Burghers, both dated 1691, but showing the progressive refinement of the design (Christ Church Library). Note the clumsy profile of the cornice as at first proposed on the left, and the improved treatment of the balustraded parapet on the right. In a letter to President Bathurst dated 2 March 1692 Wren criticises the first engraved design, in

particular the exiguous 'pinnacles' that do not stand correctly above the pilasters, and sends drawings to improve both them and the cornice. But in general he thinks the design 'is very well' and understands that the work is in any case 'too far advanced to admitt of any advice'.

28. Trinity College Chapel as built in 1691-4.

cornice) make it difficult to believe that it was due to Aldrich, but (like Wren) he may well have helped to improve the elevations and the richly decorated interior may also have benefited from his advice.

At Queen's College the building of the new library in 1693–6 is unfortunately not adequately documented. It was, as Celia Fiennes noted when she visted Oxford in about 1695 and saw it 'all new', 'a stately building emulating that of Christ Church [she meant Trinity College] in Cambridge', but no contemporary writer records the authorship of the design. The principal elevation (fig. 29) bears a general resemblance to one of the subordinate features of Wren's grand design for rebuilding Whitehall Palace after the fire of 1698 (*Wren Society*, vol. VIII, pl. viii). This might suggest that the design had originated in Wren's office but for the existence (in Aldrich's collection, now at Christ Church) of an engraving dated 1693 showing that in its original form it was a decidedly jejune composition whose pediment stood awkwardly against the attic without either entablature or pilasters to support it (fig. 30). For this first design neither Wren nor Aldrich can well have been responsible, but as the fault was corrected in execution someone

29. Queen's College Library as built in 1693–6. The open arcade on the ground floor was enclosed in 1843–5.

30. Queen's College: engraved design for the library dated 1693 (Christ Church Library).

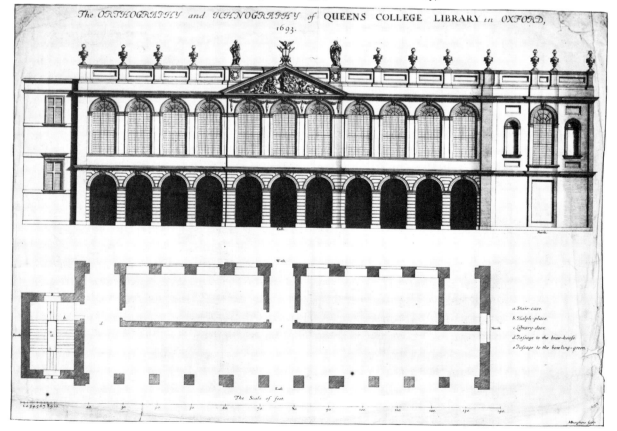

must have criticised and perhaps revised it, and in the circumstances that person is most likely to have been Aldrich.

Aldrich's successor as Oxford's architectural adviser was Dr. George Clarke (1661-1736). He was the son of Sir William Clarke, Secretary at War to Charles II, and was educated at Brasenose College. In 1680 he was elected to a fellowship at All Souls, where he 'showed brisk parts in the examination'. His political career began in 1685, when he was elected Member of Parliament for the University. He subsequently held several government posts, including those of Secretary at War, Secretary to Prince George of Denmark, and joint Secretary to the Admiralty. In 1710 he was made a Lord of the Admiralty. After the death of Queen Anne he held no further office and retired to Oxford. Here he became known as a virtuoso and man of taste and immediately took Aldrich's place as the leading architectural authority. That Clarke was a close friend of Aldrich is evident from the inscription on the monument which he erected to the latter's memory in the cathedral, and his architectural activity, like Aldrich's, had a strong scholarly basis. His extensive library (now at Worcester College) was rich in architectural works, and he acquired and studied a large portion of the surviving drawings of Inigo Jones and his pupil John Webb. Although he lacked Aldrich's facility as a draughtsman, Clarke knew how to use his rule and compasses, and his sketches often formed the basis of more finished drawings by the various architects with whom he was associated. Chief among these was Nicholas Hawksmoor, who became his constant collaborator and who probably owed his introduction to Oxford to Clarke. Like Aldrich, Clarke was much involved in the design and production of the University Almanacks and it was due to him that from 1714 onwards their pictorial headings became a regular vehicle for the illustration of new or projected buildings. For the next forty years, in fact, the Oxford Almanacks provide a gallery of unbuilt Oxford buildings - by no means all of which can be illustrated or discussed in this book.

Clarke's long association with Oxford (he held his fellowship at All Souls for more than fifty years) coincided with a period of intensive building activity that went on into the 1740s. Two important additions - the Clarendon Building and the Radcliffe Library - were made to the public buildings of the university. In the colleges almost every year saw the beginning of some new architectural project, and during the 1720s major works were simultaneously in progress at All Souls, Christ Church, Queen's and Worcester. Much of this building was made possible by private benefactions. At Christ Church the Peckwater Quadrangle was paid for largely by a bequest of £3,000 from one of the canons. At All Souls the Codrington Library commemorates the name of Christopher Codrington, a wealthy landowner in Barbados, who left £6,000 for its erection. The munificence of Dr. Radcliffe paid not only for the library which bears his name but also for a new quadrangle at University College. And at Worcester College the new buildings benefited from a legacy of £3,000 from Dr. Clarke himself. But the raising of money was often a difficult task, involving such expedients as the suspension of gaudies or even the temporary suppression of a fellowship. Queen's and Worcester both took half a century to build, at Magdalen the New Building represents only

34

the first stage of an over-ambitious scheme for rebuilding the entire college, and all that Balliol ever realised of the grand design illustrated in the Almanack of 1742 (fig. 110) was the rebuilding in 1738-43 of the eastern half of the Broad Street front, which for over a century remained in incongruous juxtaposition with the surviving medieval gate-tower (fig. 111). Many schemes were therefore mooted which were never brought to fruition, and Dr. Clarke's portfolios in Worcester College Library are full of projects that either came to nothing or were only partially realised. Some of these will be described and illustrated in the following pages.

1. All Souls College

All Souls illustrates very clearly the lack of accommodation which the building schemes of the eighteenth century were designed to remedy. Here, according to the founder's statutes, the eight senior fellows were each to share one of the eight best rooms in the college with one companion, while the remaining twenty-four fellows were to be disposed by threes in eight other rooms. The Warden had two rooms on the first floor at the south-east corner, one of which was dignified by an oriel window.

These arrangements were good enough for medieval dons, who were comparatively humble clerks of limited means who hoped sooner or later to move off to a benefice, but were not likely to satisfy the fellows of the late seventeenth and early eighteenth centuries, most of whom (particularly at All Souls, by now a distinctly aristocratic college) would have regarded themselves as gentlemen. The universities had in fact been going up in the social scale. This was true not only of the dons but also of their pupils. From the latter half of the sixteenth century onwards it became increasingly fashionable for sons of gentry, and even for some sons of noblemen, to be educated at the universities (rather than at the Inns of Court), and they naturally expected something better than a camp-bed in the rooms of a tutor who was very likely their social inferior. The medieval practice of sharing rooms – 'chumming' as it was called – was no longer acceptable, and much of the new building of the seventeenth and eighteenth centuries was designed to cater for the influx of gentlemen commoners, who demanded individual accommodation and were prepared to pay for it. Some colleges, however, for one reason or another, failed to build in the seventeenth century, and merely made the best of their existing buildings by adding attics or 'cocklofts'. One of these was All Souls, whose buildings remained essentially as Archbishop Chichele had planned them in the fifteenth century (fig. 31A).

In 1703 Dr. Clarke took the initiative by offering to build a house for himself within the precincts of the college on the understanding that it would revert to the college after his death. This eventually resulted in the building of the existing Warden's Lodgings facing the High Street, but a site adjoining the cloister which then ran alongside Catte Street was also considered and this developed into a scheme for a new north quadrangle containing twelve sets of rooms for fellows,

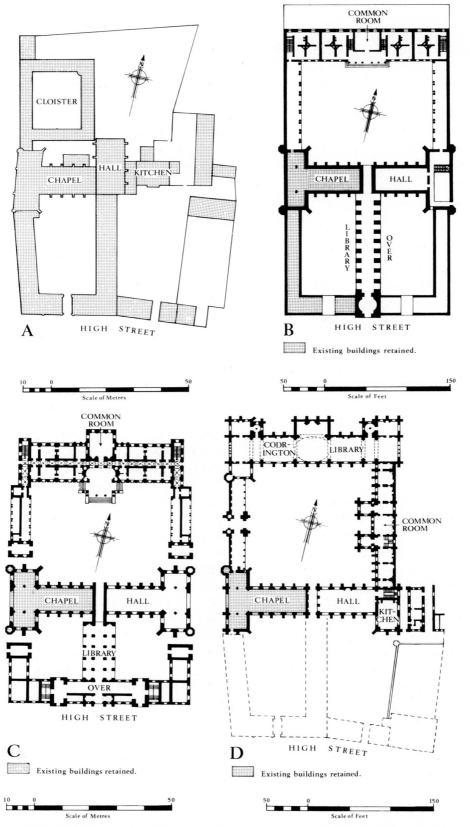

31. All Souls College: A. plan of the medieval college as existing *circa* 1700. B. The master plan made by Dr. Clarke, *circa* 1705. C. Plan by Nicholas Hawksmoor, *circa* 1708. D. Plan by Nicholas Hawksmoor, *circa* 1715 (drawn by Daphne Hart).

linked to a regularised old quadrangle by colonnades. In addition the medieval hall, anomalously placed at right angles to the chapel, was to be demolished and rebuilt in conformity to the normal Oxford plan, while a new library was to be built on arches in the front quadrangle in such a way as to provide a covered way from the entrance gateway to the new northern quadrangle (fig. 31B).

The basic plan was Clarke's, but for the new residential block different elevational treatments were made by Dean Aldrich, Nicholas Hawksmoor, John Talman, the Oxford master-mason William Townesend, and a London master-builder called Wilcox (figs. 32–8). Clarke made two designs himself, one with a giant order of a simple character, the other an essay in the Palladian manner based on one of John Webb's drawings (for Cobham Hall, Kent) in his own collection (fig. 35). Aldrich envisaged a grand Corinthian portico, Townesend a clumsy Doric one, while Wilcox submitted an old-fashioned elevation in the Wren manner with a hipped roof (he was a carpenter by trade). By far the most interesting designs were those produced by John Talman and Nicholas Hawksmoor.

Talman was the son of William Talman, formerly Comptroller of the Royal Works and the architect of Chatsworth House. He spent much of his life travelling abroad and making what the inscription on his tomb calls 'a fine collection of the most curious paintings and drawings of the noblest buildings and curiosities'. He was therefore a connoisseur architect and could be relied upon to contribute something rather different from the insular baroque of men like Hawksmoor and Townesend. Indeed, with its oval staircase hall and jaunty pediments, his proposal suggests the Piedmontese baroque of Guarino Guarini and in particular the Palazzo Carignano in Turin (pl. 1). Talman's invention did not stop at the new building, but included a remarkable scheme for rebuilding the hall in an idiosyncratic style which, as he pointed out, would be 'unlike any other in Oxford and pretty much after the Italian Gothick'. The exterior was to be decorated with a most elaborate iconographical programme which included a statue of the Founder flanked by two 'Romish' bishops in mitres and by two 'Reformed' bishops 'in their habits', thus commemorating the long history of the college as a place of ecclesiastical learning (pl. 2). The interior of the hall was likewise to be Italianate in character, with statues of successive wardens in niches round the walls, 'grotesche' decorative painting on the vaulted ceiling, and on one wall a great baroque wall-painting of the Muses surrounding Apollo, who is sitting in a round temple 'from whence he orders divers Præmiums to be distributed to multitudes of students in their proper habits (whose faces are to be from the life)' (fig. 36). It is unlikely that this exotic architectural fantasy was seriously considered by the fellows, and it was not until the nineteenth century that, under Ruskin's influence, Oxford was introduced to Italian Gothic of a somewhat different kind.

Then in 1708 or 1709 Hawksmoor came forward with a series of proposals in his most grandiloquent baroque manner. As architectural compositions they are superb, but they seem to be designed for heroes rather than for mere fellows of an Oxford college. In one a great portico spreads itself over half the façade, flanked by doorways dressed up like the entrances to some fortified town (fig. 38). In

32. All Souls College: design for new building attributed to Dean Aldrich, *circa* 1705 (Worcester College Library, no. 30).

33. All Souls College: design for new building by William Townsend, *circa* 1705 (Worcester College Library, no. 21).

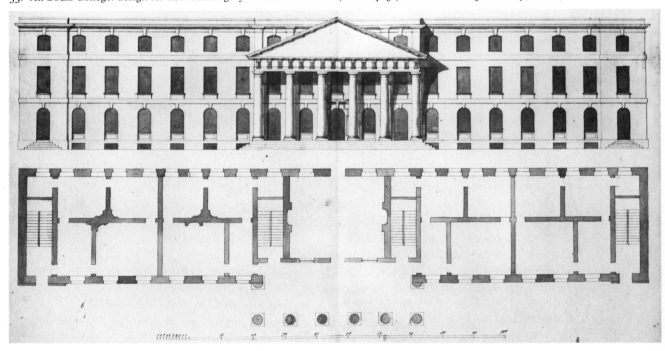

another the portico is less assertive, but the emphasis on the centre is maintained by an arched attic which, although of no practical use, would have risen above the roofs of Oxford as a dramatic and picturesque feature comparable to the steeples of Hawksmoor's London churches or the open towers of Blenheim Palace (fig. 37). If we look at the plan (fig. 31C) we see that the end bays were designed to house staircases giving access to all the rooms by means of a spinal corridor – an innovation in collegiate planning which also had its counterpart at Blenheim.

At the same time Hawksmoor prepared some equally grandiose designs for a

38

34. (*facing page, above*) All Souls College: design for new building by Edward Wilcox, *circa* 1705 (Worcester College Library, no. 52).
35. (*facing page, below*) All Souls College: design for new building by Dr. George Clarke, *circa* 1705 (Worcester College Library, no. 79).

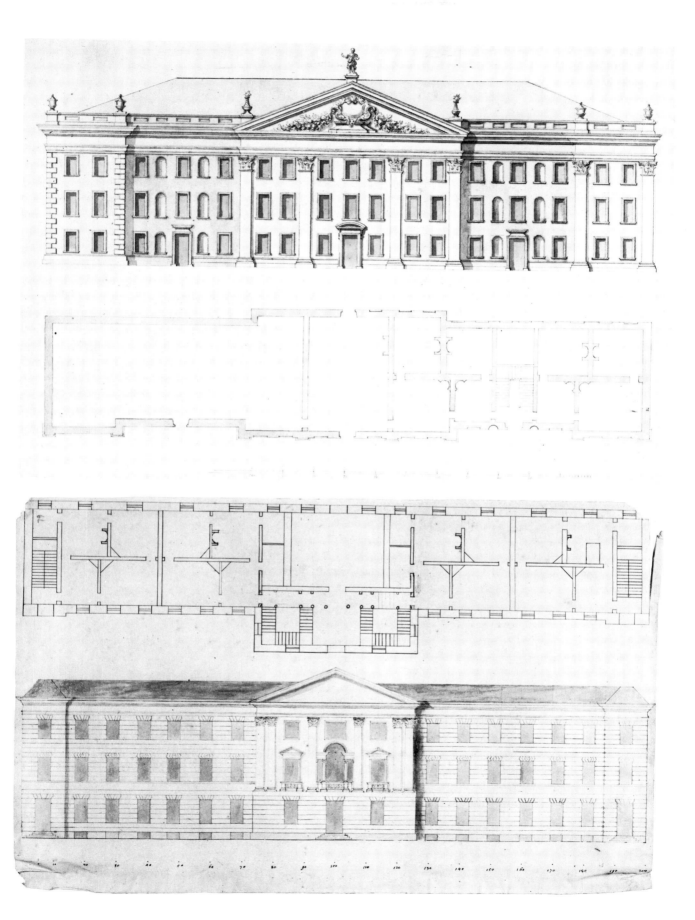

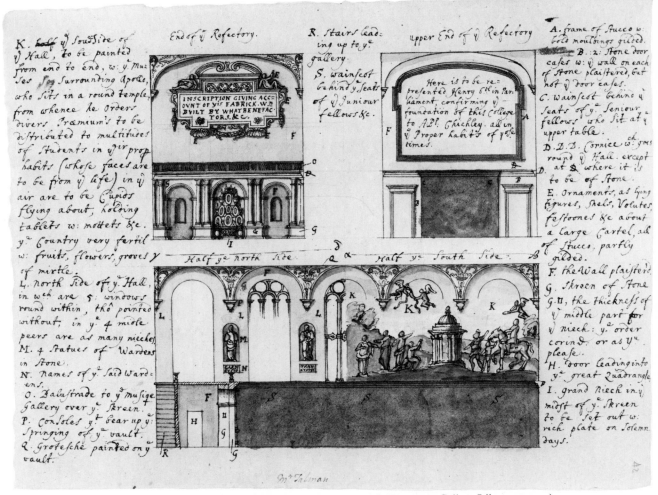

36. All Souls College: design for decoration of the hall by John Talman, 1708 (Worcester College Library, no. 42).

new High Street front surmounted by a domed tempietto of the Corinthian order (fig. 39). But soon he was envisaging a Gothic alternative with round-headed windows of a kind that had been used by Hugh May at Windsor Castle in the time of Charles II (fig. 40). There their deep, simply-moulded reveals had been found to consort well with ancient walls despite their lack of any overt Gothic detailing.

All these were colleges in the air. But in 1710 the situation was transformed by a spectacular legacy. Christopher Codrington, a *quondam* fellow who was the proprietor of large estates in the West Indies, left the college £6,000 to build a library and £4,000 to buy books. The emphasis was now on the library, for which money was immediately available, rather than on the hall and 'Grand Dormitory', for which funds would have to be found by the college. Nothing could, however, be done immediately, as an Act of Parliament was needed to enable the college to

40

secure its title to some of the ground it intended to take in to the north. By 1715 – the date when the site would be available – another consideration had to be borne in mind – one that was very much in Hawksmoor's mind: the new quadrangle would adjoin the chosen site (from 1714 onwards) of Dr. Radcliffe's library. Instead of forming one side of a narrow street, the new buildings of All Souls could now be formally related to an important square containing what promised to be the most monumental building in Oxford. The basic scheme was therefore changed: there would be a library on the north side of the new quadrangle and lodgings on the east, while the west side would be closed by a screen that would be as much an ornament to the Radcliffe Square as to the college. The change of axis from north-south to east-west (fig. 31D) was crucial for the style as well as the planning of the new quadrangle, for now the library would have to balance the chapel, and that meant that externally at least it would have to be Gothic and not classic.

In 1715 Hawksmoor accordingly submitted a new scheme on these lines, accompanied by a long 'Explanation'.* With the possible exception of the gateway to the Radcliffe Square (an ambivalent feature which might be 'after the Roman order', in order, presumably, to harmonise with the Radcliffe Library) (fig. 41), the new quadrangle was now to be entirely in the Gothic style, and as much as possible of the old quadrangle was to be preserved, though the rebuilding of the hall in line with the chapel would, of course, imply the corresponding enlargement of the quadrangle and the demolition of its eastern range to make way for the covered walk which Hawksmoor still envisaged despite the removal of the library to the north quadrangle. This delightful conceit – in effect a free-standing cloister open on both sides – can be seen in its Gothic dress in plate 3.

On 19 February 1715 the College agreed 'that the Library of Coll. Codrington should be built as the College Chappell was, according to the Model [i.e. the design] that was then showne to the Society, and that Dr. Clarke and Sir Nathaniel Lloyd be desired, to be inspectors, and take care of the sayd buildings'. The contract for the library and for the first stage of the east side of the quadrangle (including the Common Room which is its central feature) was signed with Townesend in 1716, but the detailed architectural treatment still remained to be settled. In particular, it took Hawksmoor some time to evolve the twin towers in the middle of the east wing (fig. 42). At first they were to be lower – Gothic versions of the towers with which Hawksmoor crowned his two churches in the east end of London, themselves classical paraphrases of medieval steeples such as Boston 'stump'. But in the end he attenuated them into two pinnacled turrets. The idea of twin towers as a centrepiece was itself unusual, the precedents being the west fronts of major churches like Westminster Abbey, whose towers Hawks-

---

* The 'Explanation' was printed by the College in 1960, together with a portfolio of the engravings made to Hawksmoor's designs in 1721, which incorporate subsequent modifications. Six drawings are referred to in the 'Explanation', of which no. 1 is in Worcester College Library (no. 70) and nos. 2 and 6 in the Bodleian (Gough Plans 7 and 8). The other three drawings are lost.

37. All Souls College: design for new building by Nicholas Hawksmoor, *circa* 1708 (Worcester College Library, no. 29).

38. All Souls College: design for new building by Nicholas Hawksmoor, *circa* 1708 (Worcester College Library, no. 25).

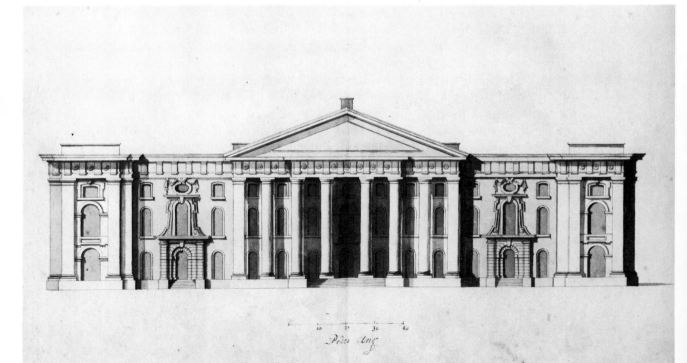

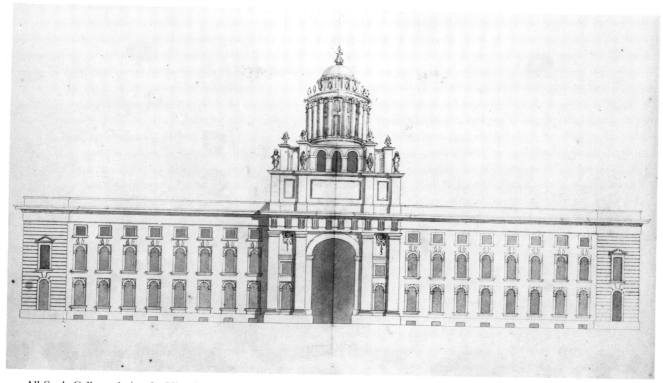

39. All Souls College: design for High Street front in the classical style by Nicholas Hawksmoor, *circa* 1708 (Worcester College Library, no. 28).

40. All Souls College: design for High Street front in the Gothic style by Nicholas Hawksmoor, *circa* 1708 (Worcester College Library, no. 131).

Pl. 3. All Souls College: Hawksmoor's design of 1715, showing the Codrington Library and new residential building more or less as execu

41. All Souls College: design for classical gateway and screen to Radcliffe Square by Nicholas Hawksmoor, 1720 (Worcester College Library, no. 5).

moor was himself to complete many years later, or Beverley Minster, which he was then engaged in repairing. But twin towers imply an entry, so one cannot help feeling a slight sense of deception when one discovers that at All Souls they do no more than stand sentinel on either side of the Common Room. From this point of view the earlier version (fig. 43) with a concave wall would perhaps have been more convincing. As it was, the Common Room assumed some architectural importance as the focal point as one looks across the quadrangle from the Radcliffe Square, and Hawksmoor produced some attractive sketches for alternative Gothic treatments, none of which were in the end carried out (fig. 44).

The Codrington Library was not completed until after Hawksmoor's death in 1736. He intended the interior to be Gothic, with a Gothic lantern rising over the central space, supported by three Gothic arches. Unfortunately there are no surviving drawings representing what would have been of especial interest as a Georgian Gothic interior earlier even than that of Horace Walpole's house at

Strawberry Hill. Dr. Clarke, however, was firmly opposed to this idea, and by 1721 it was accepted that the interior was to be classical. The existing decoration was carried out after Hawksmoor's death, and does not represent his intentions, which provided for a compartmented ceiling with much more pronounced divisions.

The hall was rebuilt in 1730–3. One of the engravings of 1721 shows the entrance at the west end, with direct access to both quadrangles, but in the event the college preferred to have the entrance at the east end, where it forms the traditional screens passage between hall and buttery. Meanwhile communication between the two parts of the college was awkwardly achieved by means of a vestibule in the north-east corner of the Front Quadrangle. Some members of the college still hoped to complete the scheme by pulling down the old eastern range and building Hawksmoor's Gothic 'columnade' to link the North Quadrangle to a new entrance gateway in the High Street front. Yet another version of this long-meditated feature was engraved by Williams in his *Oxonia Depicta* of 1732–3. But enthusiasm was waning; Codrington's money was spent, and a good deal more besides, and so when Hawksmoor died in 1736 Sir Nathaniel Lloyd, who had once thought of paying for the 'columnade', told the college that, in his opinion, 'Hawksmoring, and Townsending, is all out for this Century'.

2. *The Queen's College and Brasenose*

Drawings in Dr. Clarke's collection make it clear that he also played an important part in the rebuilding of Queen's College, projected in 1708 or 1709, the first stage of which was carried out by William Townesend between 1710 and 1721. Here, as elsewhere, the final design cannot be regarded as the exclusive work of any one individual. Clarke drew outline plans and elevations which form the basis of the existing hall, chapel and front quadrangle, and Townesend carried them out with modifications of his own. At an early stage Clarke envisaged the hall and chapel, separated by a central gateway, forming the street front of the college, but in another drawing he indicated the plan eventually adopted, with a screen wall to the street, and the hall and chapel occupying the north side of the principal quadrangle. The only part of the college that can be regarded as Hawksmoor's is the entrance screen, built by Townesend in 1733–6 and modified in execution to accommodate a statue of Queen Caroline by Henry Cheere (fig. 45). All Hawksmoor's other designs for Queen's were of so visionary and grandiose a character that their execution can never have been seriously contemplated. They show, moreover, a disregard for the established conventions of collegiate architecture that it would certainly have been difficult to accept, even if they had not been obviously far too expensive to carry out. As architectural fantasies on the theme of an Oxford college they are nevertheless well worth studying. Altogether there are eight of them, each representing a different idea that is not worked out in full but which might have been developed further had it received any support. In three of them hall and chapel are in more or less their traditional relationship,

42. All Souls College: Hawksmoor's twin towers as built (from Malton's 'Views of Oxford', 1802).

43. All Souls College, an early version of Hawksmoor's design for the twin towers, with a concave wall between them (Bodleian Library, MS. Gough Plans 8).

44. All Souls College: a sketch by Hawksmoor for the Common Room window (Worcester College Library, no. 371).

though in one (following Dr. Clarke) Hawksmoor put them on the street front, and in another he pushed them apart and then linked them together by a hemicycle of columns four deep with an archway in the middle through which could be seen a circular temple attached to the north range of the North Quadrangle (fig. 46). The result would have been a perspective worthy of Bernini or Bibiena. In three of the remaining plans (figs. 47–51) the chapel is separated from the hall to occupy a site in the middle of the quadrangle – a position for which the only precedents were the chapels of two Cambridge colleges, Peterhouse and Emmanuel. Hawksmoor's chapels, oval, peripteral, or as grandly portico'd as St. George's Bloomsbury, would, however, have looked more in place in colonnaded Ephesus or Palmyra than in an English university town.

The same might be said of Hawksmoor's schemes for Brasenose and Magdalen Colleges. The Brasenose designs are described below (p. 151). They envisage that extension of the college southwards to the High Street which was finally achieved by T. G. Jackson in 1881–9. In one of them a detached chapel once more forms the centrepiece of the principal quadrangle, while in another, made in 1734, a colonnaded 'Atrium or Corinthian peristylium' (intended, presumably, to recall Palladio's reconstruction of the Roman house as described by Vitruvius) has been introduced to give an 'antique desposition' to a smaller area carved out between the old quadrangle and the backs of the houses facing onto the High Street (fig. 157). As for the 'Scizza' for Magdalen which Hawksmoor sent to Dr. Clarke in 1724 (fig. 84), it would have turned its Gothic quadrangles into a complex of hemicycles, atriums, vestibules and porticos more like an imperial villa than a traditional Oxford college.

50

45. Queen's College: the High Street front, showing the entrance screen built in 1733–6 substantially in accordance with Hawksmoor's designs.

3. Christ Church Library

While the first stages of All Souls and Queen's were under way, Dr. Clarke and William Townesend were also engaged in building a monumental library at Christ Church. This took the place of the detached residential block envisaged by Aldrich, and was at first intended to conform externally to his design. A legacy from Dr. Robert South enabled the work to start in 1717. 'We have got the £500 which Dr. South left us to our building, and shall pull down the last side of Peckwater next spring', wrote Canon Stratford to Edward Harley in September 1716, '... we shall observe Dr. Aldrich's model as to the case, but we design to turn the inside into a library, and to make it the finest library that belongs to any society in Europe'. Although Aldrich's giant Corinthian order was retained, the change of use enabled Clarke to eliminate the attic windows and to reduce the number of bays from nine to seven. After several experiments with fenestration

51

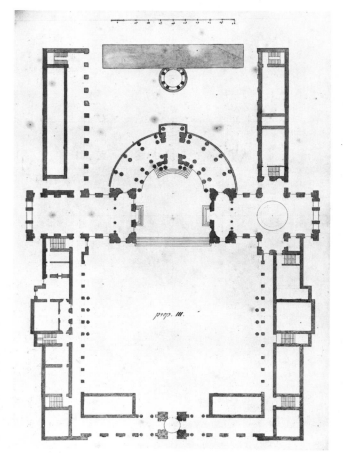

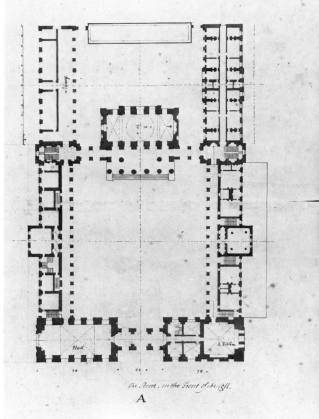

46. (*above left*) Queen's College: design by Nicholas Hawksmoor for a college with hall and cruciform chapel separated by a columned hemicycle with a view through to a tempietto (Queen's College archives).

47. (*above right*) Queen's College: design by Nicholas Hawksmoor for a college with hall and kitchen on the street front and chapel separating the two quadrangles (Queen's College archives).

48. Queen's College: *above*, elevation of the chapel as in fig. 47, with flanking towers surmounting the two staircases: *below*, elevation of the street front as in fig. 47 (Queen's College archives).

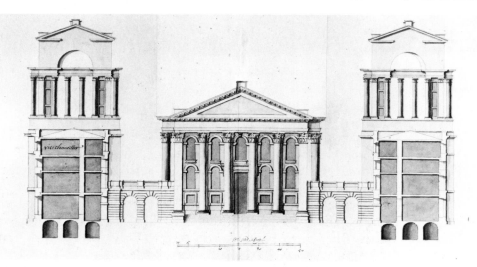

52

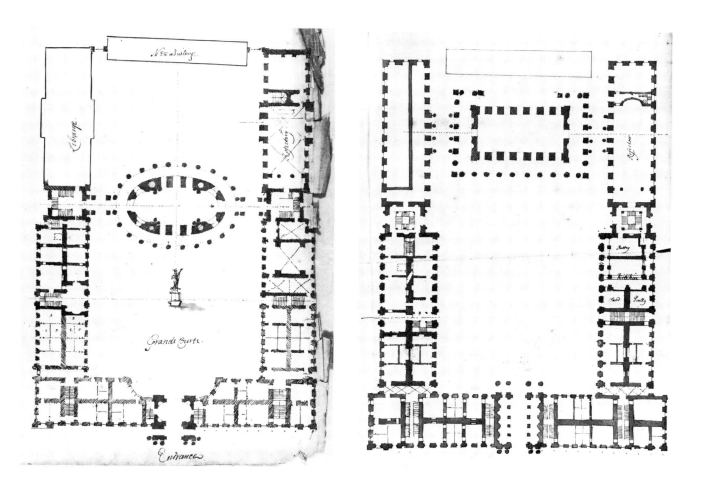

49. (*above left*) Queen's College: design by Hawksmoor for a college with oval chapel separating the two quadrangles and hall opposite the library (Queen's College archives).

50. (*above right*) Queen's College: design by Hawksmoor for a college with one large quadrangle dominated by a chapel in the form of a rectangular temple. The hall is on the right, occupying the site of the Williamson Building, and balancing the library on the left (Queen's College archives).

51. Queen's College: sketch by Hawksmoor for a version of the oval chapel as in fig. 49 (Queen's College archives).

of a Palladian character (one of which is illustrated in figure 52), Clarke finally worked out a façade whose organisation derives from Michelangelo's Capitoline Palace in Rome (fig. 53). The interior, with its fine joinery and exquisite plaster-work by Roberts, was not completed until 1762, and in 1769 the ground floor, hitherto open on three sides, was enclosed in order to house the collection of pictures bequeathed by General John Guise. Altogether this splendid building had cost the college £15,000.

4. Worcester College

The last college to benefit from Dr. Clarke's architectural advice was the new foundation of Worcester. In disgust at the quarrels which rent his own college, it was to Worcester that he eventually left not only his library and architectural drawings, but also the bulk of his fortune, part of which was to be devoted to the completion of its buildings. The new hall, chapel and library had already been begun in his lifetime, and the basic design seems to have been his. Though the elevational treatment was unadventurous, the placing of hall and chapel on either side of the recessed entrance and the prominence given to the library were well-conceived innovations in planning that were without precedent in Oxford's collegiate architecture. Here, as at All Souls, Hawksmoor was once more Clarke's architectural adjutant, and a number of drawings exist to illustrate their collaboration. Many of these relate to the fenestration of the library, for which various ideas were considered, some of them 'Palladian' in character. The final solution of three arched windows with pilastered jambs was derived (as an annotation of Hawksmoor's shows) from the Roman arch at Saintes, as illustrated in Blondel's *Cours d'architecture* of 1698. Another 'antique' feature proposed by Hawksmoor that was not adopted was a pair of octagonal turrets (one containing the chapel bell) professedly derived from the 'Tower of the Winds' at Athens, a building of which accurate drawings were not then available, but whose general form was known from a passage in Vitruvius. Paul Draper's drawing (fig. 54) shows how the front of Worcester would have appeared from Beaumont Street had Hawksmoor's designs been adopted.

To complete the college Dr. Clarke envisaged two wings projecting westwards to north and south of the library with a new lodging for the Provost at the west end of the northern wing. This proposal was published by Williams in his *Oxonia Depicta* of 1732-3, and in his will Clarke directed that the new north range should be commenced in accordance with the engraving (fig. 55). But finding that there was not sufficient room for the building as originally envisaged between the library and the old Provost's Lodgings, he left instructions in a codicil that an alternative plan and elevation, which he had initialled, should be followed instead. This drawing has not survived, but a comparison between the 1732 plan and the building as erected shows that the residential range has been thickened from a 'single' to a 'double pile', thus enabling the smaller rooms to be placed at the rear. In this form the two easternmost staircases on the north side were duly erected by

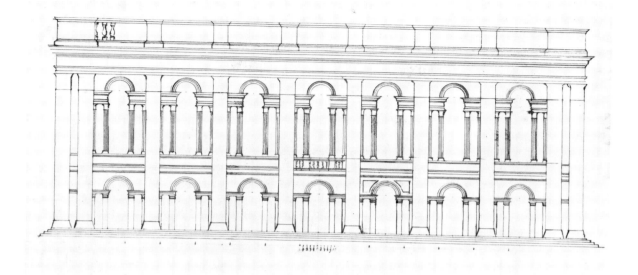

52. Christ Church: one of Dr. Clarke's alternative designs for the Library, using the motif of the Palladian window (Christ Church Library).

53. Christ Church: engraving of the Library essentially as built, but with alternative treatments of the ground floor shown to right and left of the central doorway (Christ Church Library).

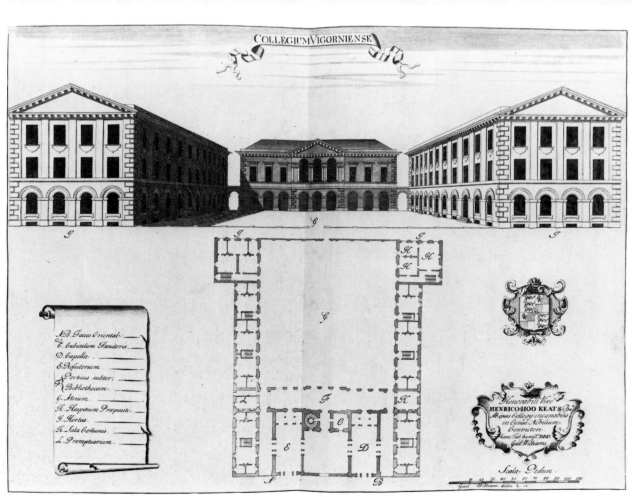

COLLEGIUM VIGORNIENSE

B. Fores Orientalis.
C. Cubiculum Janitoris.
D. Capella.
E. Refectorium.
F. Porticus subter Bibliothecam.
G. Atrium.
H. Hospitium Præpositi.
I. Hortus.
K. Sala Communis.
L. Promptuarium.

Honorabili Viro
HENRICO HOO KEATS B.
hujus collegii incunabula
in Censu Nobilium
Convictoris
hanc Tab. humill: D.D.D.
Guil: Williams

Scala Pedum.

Guil: Williams delin: s: sc:

54. (*facing page, above*) Worcester College: the front as envisaged by Hawksmoor, a perspective drawing by Paul Draper based on drawings in Worcester College Library (nos. 465, 467).

55. (*facing page, below*) Worcester College: engraving from William's *Oxonia Depicta* (1732) showing the complete design as intended by Dr. Clarke. The south wing (seen on the right in the perspective, and on the left in the plan) was never built, and the Provost's Lodging at the west end of the north wing was eventually built to a different, though compatible, design.

56. Worcester College: the north range as built between 1753 and 1776.

57. Worcester College: the entrance front as exposed to view by the construction of Beaumont Street in the 1820s (from an engraving in Ryman's *Illustrations of Oxford*, 1839).

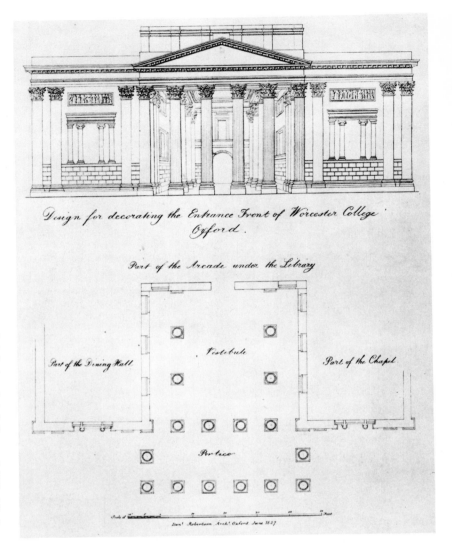

Design for decorating the Entrance Front of Worcester College Oxford.

Part of the Arcade under the Library

Part of the Dining Hall   *Vestibule*   *Part of the Chapel*

Portico

Dan.ᵗ Robertson Arch.ᵗ Oxford June 1827

58. Worcester College: Daniel Robertson's design for remodelling the entrance front in the 'Grecian style', 1827 (Worcester College Library, no. 493).

59. (*facing page, above*) Worcester College: Charles Barry's design for remodelling the entrance front in the Italianate style, 1827 (Worcester College Library, no. 503).

60. (*facing page, below*) Worcester College: anonymous design for improving the entrance front, undated but based on the view of the college by J. M. W. Turner in the *Oxford Almanack* for 1804 (Worcester College Library, no. 492).

Dr. Clarke's trustees between 1753 and 1759. The remainder of the north range, including the Provost's Lodgings, was built between 1773 and 1776 to modified designs by Henry Keene (fig. 56). The corresponding range on the south side was never built, and it was not until 1783-4 that the interiors of the hall and chapel received their elegant neo-classical decoration at the hands of James Wyatt.

Remotely situated in what was then a back street, Worcester was only brought visually into relationship with the rest of the university by the cutting through of Beaumont Street early in the 1820s (fig. 57). This gave the plain recessed front a new prominence, and it was soon suggested that it should be made to live up to its new consequence by the insertion of an archway or a colonnade between the wings. Daniel Robertson showed what could be done with Grecian, and Charles Barry with Italianate, trimmings (figs. 58, 59), but the most attractive scheme is perhaps an anonymous one for a pedimented aedicule surmounted by an unidentified statue (fig. 60).

58

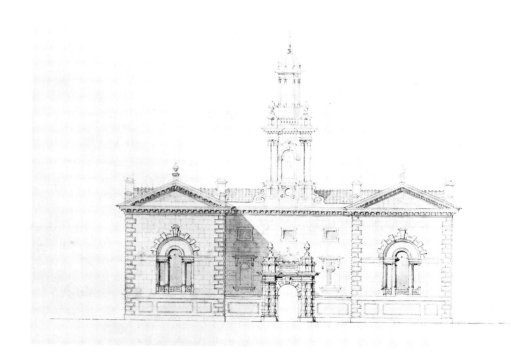

V

Hawksmoor's Oxford

A SUBSIDIARY FUNCTION of the Sheldonian Theatre was to house the University Press. The compositors worked under the galleries, the presses were accommodated in the basement, and the books and sheets were stored in the attic. But the arrangements were highly inconvenient for all concerned, and some anxiety was felt about the effect on the roof-trusses of the dead weight of books and paper which they supported.

However the publication in 1702-4 of Clarendon's *History of the Rebellion* was so profitable that the Delegates of the University Press were able to contemplate the erection of a new printing house designed for the purpose. A site was found in Broad Street, and designs were obtained from at least three architects, namely Nicholas Hawksmoor, John James and William Townesend. The original drawings are all in Dr. Clarke's collection, and it is evident that he was closely involved in an advisory capacity.

Hawksmoor was given the commission (for which he received a single payment of £100), and the superiority of his designs can easily be seen from a comparison of figures 61-7. Nevertheless John James was a competent architect and the elegant precision of the elevation which he submitted was characteristic of his architectural draughtsmanship. It was also characteristic of him to offer a design that, although it must be classified as 'baroque', is of a relatively sober and conventional character (fig. 61). In 1711 he was to assure the Duke of Buckingham that his ambition was to show 'that the Beautys of Architecture may consist with the greatest plainness of the structure', something that he claimed 'has scarce ever been hit on by the Tramontani unless by our famous Mr. Inigo Jones'. Had he been born a few years later he would doubtless have been a recruit to the new Palladianism. The design attributed to William Townesend (d. 1739),* the leading Oxford master-mason of his day, is much less accomplished but would have looked better in execution than it does drawn out in Townesend's rather clumsy hand (fig. 62). Seal's coffee-house on the site of the Indian Institute was a humbler building in the same style for which Townesend was probably responsible.

---

* It is in the same hand as a design for All Souls in Dr. Clarke's collection marked 'Young Mr. Townesend's design'.

60

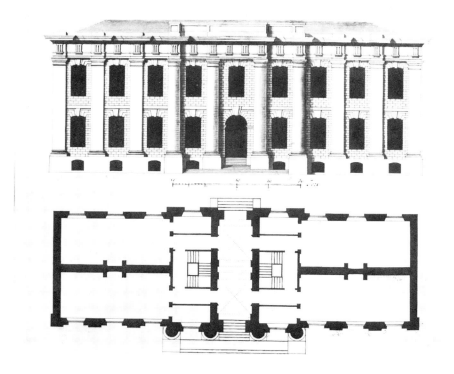

61. The Clarendon Building: design attributed to John James (Worcester College Library, no. 111).

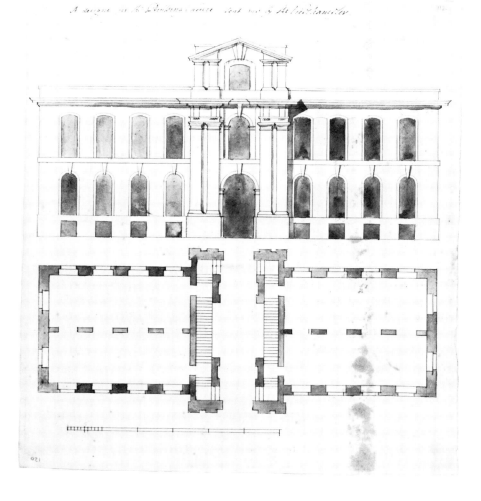

62. The Clarendon Building: design attributed to William Townesend (Worcester College Library, no. 120).

63, 64. The Clarendon Building: alternative designs by Nicholas Hawksmoor (Worcester College Library, nos. 112, 115).

62

65, 66. The Clarendon Building: alternative designs by Nicholas Hawksmoor (Worcester College Library, nos. 113, 114).

After Hawksmoor's death 'Fourteen Designs of Printing and Town Houses [i.e. Town Halls] of Oxford by Mr. Hawksmoor' were offered for sale by his executors. These have not come to light, but five alternative elevations for the Clarendon Building (as the printing house was to be called) are preserved in Dr. Clarke's collection. They cannot be arranged in any sequence and evidently do not represent the progressive evolution of a finished design from a first idea. They are alternatives of equal validity and since they are all intended to fit essentially the same ground-plan they serve once more to illustrate the remarkable fertility of Hawksmoor's invention. In all of them he has sought an effect of monumental gravity by the use of a Doric order against walls heavy with keystones or deeply shadowed by recession. Unlike John James, the centre of whose façade is in equipoise between equally balanced wings, Hawksmoor has sought to create that tension which is one of the essences of baroque composition. In figure 63 this is produced, as Professor Downes has pointed out, by reversing the conventional functions of portico and pediment. The pediment, instead of crowning the portico, is enormously enlarged to embrace the whole building, while the portico projects in front merely as a pedestal for a group of statues. In figure 64 the portico is cleft in half by a recess, so that the visual integrity of the building is maintained only by the fenestration and the Doric order that is threaded through the pilasters at first floor level. In figure 66 it is the fenestration that is centrifugal and the portico that binds together the two halves of the façade. In the building as executed in 1712–15 the portico is conventional and the elevations are enlivened by the variations in the spacing of the central windows and by the alternate recession and projection of the wall surface on either side (fig. 67). The roofline is animated by lead statues of the Muses designed, probably at Clarke's behest, by Sir James Thornhill.

*   *   *

The Radcliffe Library is one of Oxford's most conspicuous architectural ornaments. It is not, however, one of Oxford's most convenient libraries, nor (especially before the enclosure of the vaulted basement in 1862) can there have been many libraries in which the number of books housed is so small in proportion to the total cubic area: in fact it would be difficult to find an Oxford building in whose design purely aesthetic considerations have been less constrained by those of cost or utility. How this came about can only be fully understood in the light of the many unexecuted designs for the building that have been preserved in the Ashmolean Museum.

Dr. John Radcliffe was the most fashionable and successful physician of his age. He lived and died a bachelor, and the university of which he was a member was the principal object of his benefactions. At least two years before his death in 1714 he expressed the intention of enlarging the Bodleian Library, and in his will he left ample funds for the purpose. His original idea was to build out from the western or Selden End of the Bodleian into the adjoining garden of Exeter College.

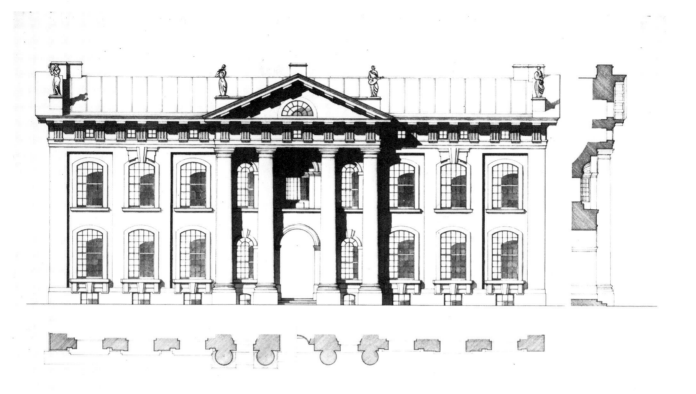

67. The Clarendon Building as built to Hawksmoor's designs in 1712-15 (from a drawing by Peter Brigham, A.R.I.B.A.).

The new library was to be ninety feet long and two stories high. The upper part was to be on the level of Duke Humfrey's Library. The ground floor was to be given to Exeter as a college library in order to compensate that society for the loss of its ground. For such a building several alternative designs were made by Hawksmoor (figs. 68-70). Some were rectangular and some circular, but all were monumental rather than utilitarian, and in so far as they had any identifiable prototypes these were temples and mausolea rather than libraries. There are indications that what Dr. Radcliffe wanted was as much a monument to himself as a useful addition to the library, and as for Hawksmoor he would have needed no encouragement to think in terms of antique grandeur. However a site in Exeter College garden was not the best calculated for a public monument, and the fellows for their part 'insisted upon such terms, as evinced their great unwillingness to lose the benefit of a good part of their garden'. So when Dr. Radcliffe made his will in September 1714 he directed that (subject to the life-interest of his two sisters) £40,000 should be devoted to 'building a library in Oxford and the purchasing the houses between St. Maries and the schools in Catstreet where I intend the library to be built'. Besides making further negotiations with Exeter

65

68. The Radcliffe Library:
design by Nicholas Hawks-
moor for the library as a
rectangular addition to the
Selden End of Duke Hum-
frey's library (Ashmolean
Museum).

69. (*below left*) The Radcliffe Library: section of
Hawksmoor's design for
the library as a circular
domed addition to the Selden End of Duke Hum-
frey's library (Ashmolean
Museum).

70. (*below right*) The Radcliffe Library: elevation of
Hawksmoor's design for
the library as a circular
domed addition to the Selden End of Duke Hum-
frey's library (Ashmolean
Museum).

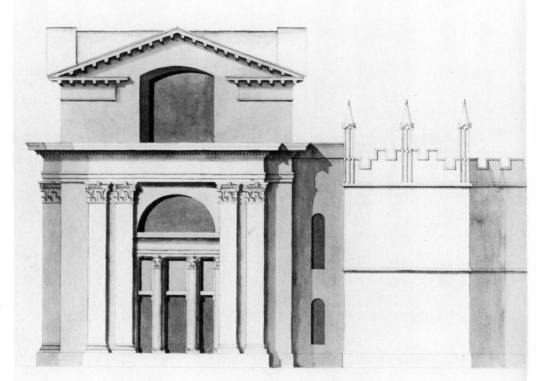

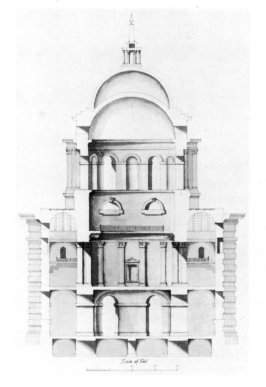

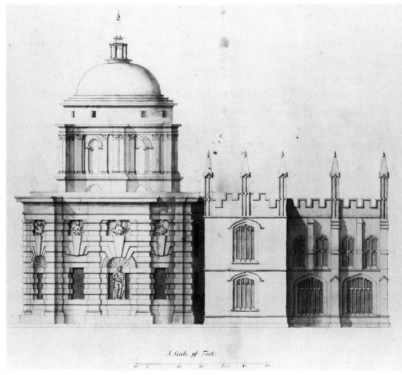

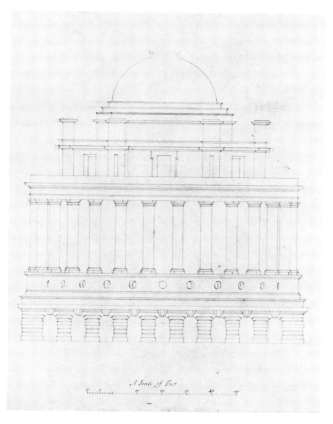

71. The Radcliffe Library: design by Hawksmoor for a circular domed library on the south side of the Schools Quadrangle (Ashmolean Museum).

72. The Radcliffe Library: Hawksmoor's sketch for a circular domed library on the south side of the Schools Quadrangle, dated 1715 (Ashmolean Museum).

unnecessary, this would give the library a much more prominent site, a consideration that may well have weighed heavily with a benefactor who (according to Hearne) was 'very ambitious of glory'. The buying up of property to clear the site was a slow process, necessitating an Act of Parliament, and it was not until 1737 that work could actually begin.

Meanwhile Hawksmoor had made fresh designs for a library on the new site: not, at this stage, one completely insulated, but connected by a vestibule to the south side of the Schools Quadrangle. It was to be a circular domed building standing on a square base of channelled masonry. In one version a peristyle of close-set Doric columns recalls the mausoleum at Castle Howard (fig. 71); in the other attached Corinthian columns and festooned circular windows produce a more genial and elegant building (figs. 72–3). Neither was to be built, but (as will be seen) both have their place in the pre-history of the existing library.

At the same time, Hawksmoor had allowed his imagination to run free in the direction of town-planning. Here, as at Cambridge, he sought to transform what was essentially a medieval street-system by the opening up of new vistas and the construction of new buildings. At Cambridge he took as his model the baroque replanning of Rome by Domenico Fontana in the time of Pope Sixtus V, but at

73. The Radcliffe Library: Hawksmoor's 1715 design as it would have been seen from the Radcliffe Square, drawn by Paul Draper.

Oxford the approximately rectilinear pattern of streets encouraged him to think in terms of a Roman city, with a *Forum Universitatis* between the Schools and St. Mary's Church, a *Forum Civitatis* at Carfax, and triumphal gateways at the north end of the Cornmarket and the east end of the High Street (fig. 74). On the west side of the University Forum a rebuilt Brasenose would answer to a rebuilt All Souls, and on the site of Hart Hall (now Hertford College) a large many-columned classical temple would serve as a '*Capella Universitatis*'. North of it a detached campanile is indicated on his plans. To the south of the Radcliffe Library the centre of the new square is marked by a statue of Queen Anne, while a column like Trajan's in Rome rises in the middle of the City Centre or *Forum Civitatis*. As town-planning it is magnificent, but the destruction of existing property would have been extensive, and the cost enormous. There are several variant versions of Hawksmoor's schemes, but there is no evidence that any of them was ever seriously considered by the university, let alone the civic authorities, and over fifty years were to elapse before town and university were to unite in achieving the much more modest urban improvements effected by the Oxford Paving Commissioners.

By 1720 the accumulation of Dr. Radcliffe's estate had encouraged his trustees to think of implementing his instructions and they resolved not only to press on

74. Hawksmoor as a town-planner. Hawksmoor's grand design for Oxford, *circa* 1712. A. new Bocardo gate. B. Turl gate. C. *Elaboratorium.* D. alternative sites for Radcliffe Library. E. Master Printer's house. F. new University Church or *Capella Universitatis.* G. campanile. H. new East Gate in the form of a triumphal arch. K. column. (Redrawn by Daphne Hart from Bodleian Library, MS. Top. Oxon. a. 26 (R).)

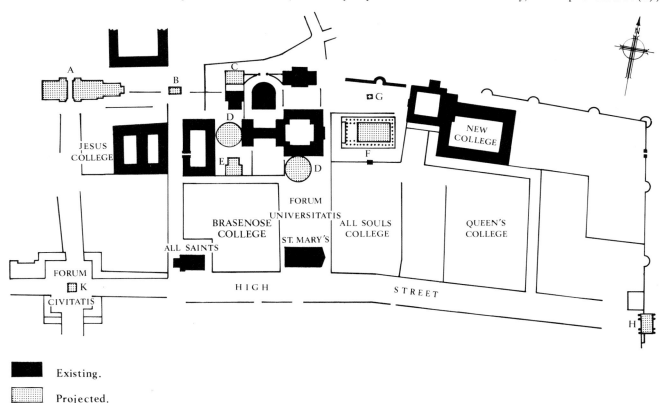

75. The Radcliffe Library: Hawksmoor's 1735 design as it would have been seen from the Radcliffe Square: a drawing by Paul Draper based on the wooden model. Some details of the dome are missing and are here conjecturally restored.

with the acquisition of the site, but to solicit designs for the library from 'the ablest architects ... vizt. such as, Sir Christopher Wren, Sir John Vanbourg, Sir James Thornhill, Mr. Archer, Mr. Hawksmore, Mr. James & Mr. Gibbs &c.' It

70

is doubtful, however, whether any approach was in fact made to architects at this date, and certainly no designs are known that can be attributed to Wren, Vanbrugh, Thornhill, Archer or James. In fact it was not until 1734 that the question of the design was taken up again. Early in the following year the trustees had before them plans submitted by Nicholas Hawksmoor and James Gibbs. Hawksmoor had by now been associated with the scheme for over twenty years. Gibbs as an architect with important buildings to his credit in London and Cambridge was an obvious choice if the trustees wanted to see some alternative designs. Moreover he was, like themselves, a staunch Tory. The two architects submitted radically different schemes. Hawksmoor once more envisaged a circular building standing on a high base of channelled masonry, but this time with rectangular pedimented windows instead of round-headed ones and a dome supported by eight prominent buttresses (fig. 75). Internally the library was compartmented into a series of radial rooms surrounding a circular central space lit from above. Gibbs offered several variant versions of a long rectangular block occupying the greater part of the new square (fig. 76). The external treatment varied from an ill-judged display of rustication on astylar walls to a Corinthian order deployed in a manner reminiscent of Wren's library at Trinity College, Cambridge (fig. 77). Internally, large rectangular rooms provided ample shelf space and there were

76. The Radcliffe Library: one of James Gibbs's plans for a rectangular library occupying nearly the whole of the area between the Schools Quadrangle (on the left) and St. Mary's Church (on the right) (Ashmolean Museum).

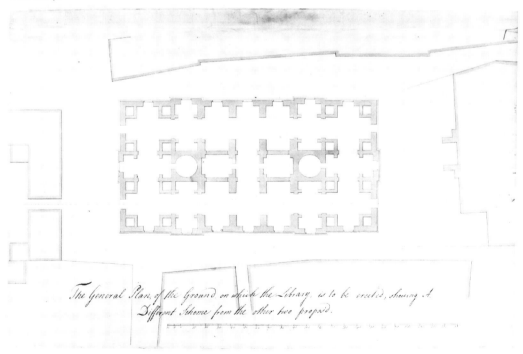

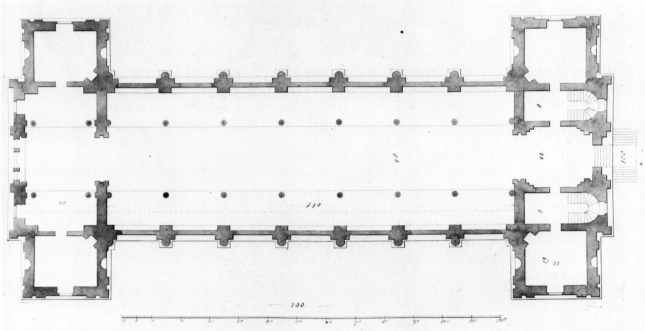

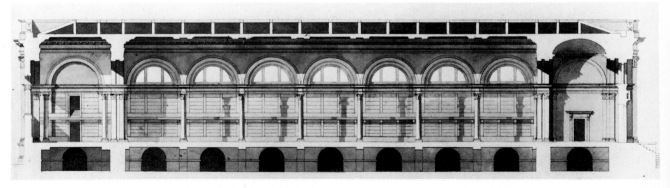

77. The Radcliffe Library: plan, section and elevation of one of James Gibbs's designs for a rectangular library (Ashmolean Museum).

smaller rooms at either end for administration or special collections. As a working library there can be no doubt that Gibbs's proposal was much the more practical. But as an embellishment to Oxford – above all as a monument to Dr. Radcliffe – Hawksmoor's domed building was calculated to make the greater effect.

The indications are that Hawksmoor's design was the one accepted, and a wooden model of it (now displayed in the City Museum) was made at the trustees' expense. But Hawksmoor's death in March 1736 left the commission in Gibbs's hands, and it was under the latter's direction that the library was built between 1737 and 1748. What Gibbs did – presumably at the trustees' desire – was to accept the theme of a circular domed building, but to interpret it in his own way. As a pupil of the Roman architect Carlo Fontana Gibbs was well acquainted with the many domed churches of Italy and the result was something more like an Italian baroque church and less like an antique mausoleum than Hawksmoor had envisaged. In the interior, he enlarged the arches supporting the cupola and removed the radial walls by which Hawksmoor had subdivided the aisles so as to create a continuous ambulatory round the periphery. In doing this he was following the example of Fontana's design for the Jesuit sanctuary at Loyola in Spain, itself in this respect influenced by Longhena's church of S. Maria della Salute in Venice. In the exterior, the coupling of the three-quarter columns, the alternation of elaborately dressed windows with less emphatic niches, and the intrusion of the former's pediments into the zone of the capitals, are all calculated to enliven the building and to create more complex visual rhythms than those inherent in Hawksmoor's simpler but more monumental design. The only weakness of the building as it stands today (fig. 78) lies in the lantern crowning the cupola, which is lighter and visually less effective than the one originally intended by the architect. This followed the decision in 1741 to substitute a timber dome for the one of stone shown in Gibbs's original designs (figs. 79–80). There is no suggestion in the trustees' minutes that this was due to any shortage of money, but no stone dome of such size had ever been built in England, and Gibbs may have had doubts about the ability of the masons to complete it successfully. A scale model of the stone dome was, however, made (itself in stone), and survives as part of an ornamental building in the garden of St. Giles' House, then the residence of Thomas Rowney, Member of Parliament for the city of Oxford (fig. 81).

The completion of the Radcliffe Library in 1748 marks the end of the building boom in early Georgian Oxford. The long delay in starting work on the library and the slow continuance, at Worcester and Queen's Colleges, of buildings begun long before meant that while elsewhere in the country Palladianism was in fashion between the Anglo-baroque of the early eighteenth century and the neo-classical architecture of the later Georgian period, in Oxford the latter followed close on the heels of the former without any intervening Palladian phase. The conduct of architecture in the university was, moreover, changing. Dean Aldrich and Dr. Clarke had no successors: the age of the amateur was over and that of the professional had arrived. During the reign of George III Oxford's architectural patronage was bestowed first on Henry Keene (d. 1776) and then on James Wyatt

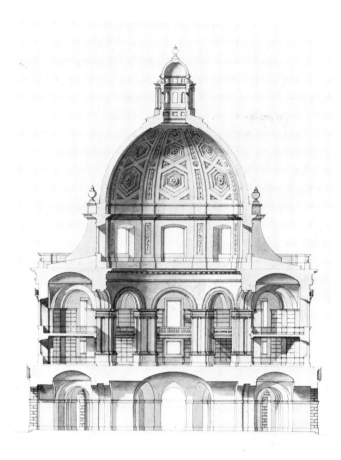

The Upright of the Building intended for the Radcliffe Library as it is seen on all sides.

78. (*facing page*) The Radcliffe Library as completed in 1748.

79, 80. (*above*) The Radcliffe Library: elevation and section of the library as begun in 1737, but with a stone dome instead of a wooden one covered with lead (Ashmolean Museum).

81. The Radcliffe Library: scale model of the stone dome and lantern in the garden of St. Giles' House, Oxford.

82. The Radcliffe Observatory. *Below*: a drawing by J. B. Malchair showing the state of the building in October 1774, eighteen months after Henry Keene had been superseded as architect by James Wyatt. On the right is the Professor of Astronomy's house, and on the left the scaffolded ground story of the main building (Corpus Christi College Library). *Above*: the completed building, a drawing by John Dixon made for the *Oxford Almanack* of 1794 (Ashmolean Museum).

(d. 1813). Keene's last building and Wyatt's first was the Radcliffe Observatory, now part of Green College. This was begun to Keene's designs in 1772, but in March of the following year he was superseded by Wyatt. None of Keene's drawings survive, but it is clear that the adjoining Professor's house was his work, and a sketch (fig. 82) made in October 1774 shows that by that date the ground floor of the main building was far advanced. There is, however, a gap in the centre for the substructure of the tower, and the whole of this important feature may therefore have been designed anew by Wyatt.

Apart from the Observatory Wyatt's principal works in Oxford in the classical style were the Canterbury Quadrangle at Christ Church (1775–8), the remodelling of the interiors of the libraries at New College (1778) and Brasenose (1779–80), the completion of the hall and chapel at Worcester College (1783 onwards), and the building of a new library at Oriel (1788–9). As a Gothic architect Wyatt demonstrated his skill by altering or remodelling the interiors of the halls of Merton (1790–1), Magdalen (1790–5) and Balliol (1792). The chapels at Magdalen and New College and the library at Balliol were also re-Gothicised under his direction, and at Christ Church he designed the staircase up to the hall and the panelling and fireplaces in the hall itself. Although some of Wyatt's Gothic work (notably in the hall at Merton and the chapel at New College) has since been undone by Victorian 'restoration', there are only one or two abortive designs by him which claim a place in this book. By far the most important are the ones for Magdalen College which are described in the following chapter.

VI

Indecision at Magdalen

MAGDALEN has a longer history of architectural indecision than any other Oxford college. Between 1720 and 1844 at least twenty architects are known to have made designs for, or been consulted by, the college, and among the mass of drawings preserved in the college library there are several by other designers not yet identified.

Here, as elsewhere, the medieval buildings were quite inadequate for the needs of the early Georgian dons and fellow-commoners, and although something had been done to ease the situation by adding 'cocklofts', some new accommodation was urgently needed. Moreover the old buildings themselves appear to have been in poor repair, and Hawksmoor may have been only slightly exaggerating when he told Dr. Clarke that Magdalen was 'a College so decriped that repairing any part (except the hall and chapell) signifys but little, so that the whole must (or ought to be) new'. As early as 1720 Hearne was told that 'they unanimously agreed at Magdalen-College to pull down and rebuild the East Side of that College', and it was in that year that one of the fellows, Dr. Edward Butler, gave one hundred guineas to start a building fund. The page of the Benefactors' Book which records Butler's gift shows the college rebuilt in the form of a great crescent, with Magdalen Tower preserved (apparently alone of the ancient buildings) to form an entrance gateway (fig. 83).* This ruthlessly simple solution may only have been a calligrapher's fancy, but it is nevertheless interesting conceptually. For the first of all crescents (the one at Bath) was not begun until 1767, so the unknown author of the Magdalen initial had anticipated John Wood's celebrated innovation in urban architecture by nearly half a century. Among the college archives there is an almost equally drastic design endorsed as 'Mr. B——'s plan'. It consists of two vast quadrangles, one incorporating the existing hall and chapel on its south side, with a new library to match the chapel on the north, the other made up of three

---

* This idea had an unconscious echo in 1947 when Magdalen contemplated pulling down the buildings of the Botanic Garden immediately opposite the college and erecting in their place a new neo-Georgian building designed by Oliver Hill. His drawings, exhibited at the Royal Academy, showed a shallow crescent divided on either side of the Danby Gate, and symmetrically related to Magdalen Tower on the other side of the road.

Pl. 4. Magdalen College: one of James Wyatt's designs for a Gothic altarpiece in the chapel, 1791 (Magdalen College Library).

83. Magdalen College: miniature drawing in the Benefactors' Book (1720) showing a scheme for rebuilding the college in the form of a crescent, preserving the tower as an entrance gateway (Magdalen College Library). This is the first suggestion of a crescent in English architecture, but the form had been used for subsidiary buildings abroad, notably at Lustheim in Bavaria (*circa* 1680).

84. (*facing page*) Magdalen College: sketch for rebuilding the college made by Nicholas Hawksmoor in 1724. The tower again serves as an entrance gateway to the buildings described on page 80 (Worcester College Library, no. 85).

identical detached blocks, each containing twenty-four sets, standing at right-angles to one another on the site of the present St Swithin's Quadrangle. Each block was to be identical in plan, and presumably in elevation, with Gibbs's New Building at King's College, Cambridge, and it is just possible that 'Mr. B——' was James Burrough, a Cambridge don then just starting on his career as an amateur architect.

Hawksmoor too gave his mind to the problem. In 1724 he sent Dr. Clarke a sketch for rebuilding the college for his 'diversion' (fig. 84). Like the unknown author of the crescent he was clearly worried by the informal relationship between the college buildings and the tower, their main architectural ornament. A hundred years later Humphry Repton would point out that in a medieval building 'the degree of irregularity seems often to have been studied, to produce grandeur by the intricacy and variety of its parts', and that at Magdalen in particular the tower appears to best advantage from the quadrangle precisely because from there it is seen obliquely rather than straight on (cf. figs. 94, 102). This was, however, an appreciation of the picturesque of which no one (with the possible exception of Vanbrugh) would have been capable in the 1720s. So all Hawksmoor's Oxford designs, however picturesque in intention, are based on classical symmetry rather than on Gothic irregularity. Here at Magdalen he gives the tower a symmetrical setting between two wings which contain hall and chapel. Pierced with arches at the base, it now serves as a grand entrance tower to the college. Beyond it one progresses through a circular vestibule into the arcaded quadrangle or 'Grand Cloyster', on the far side of which rises the library, raised on vaulted arches. From the tower there is a grand vista through the vestibule, past an obelisk, across the quadrangle and under the library to a smaller quadrangle or 'Corinthian Atrium'

80

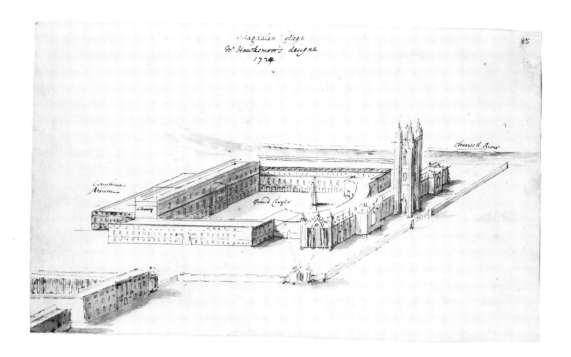

and so out to the park. The street front is Gothic, to match the tower, but all the rest is grandly classical. 'If it was drawne fair', Hawksmoor told Dr. Clarke, 'it would shew the beauty of the ancient building (as Col. Campbell says in his Workes) in the Vitruvian Style.'

This, of course, was a mere sketch made by Hawksmoor for his own and Dr. Clarke's pleasure and never seriously considered by the college, if indeed it was ever shown to them. For the design that was actually adopted the college was indebted to Edward Holdsworth, a talented classical scholar and connoisseur of the arts whose refusal to accept the religious supremacy of the Hanoverian dynasty has cost him his fellowship in 1715, but who had remained in close touch with his former colleagues. In 1720 a survey of the college was made for his use, but it was not until 1728 that the fellows were in a position to contemplate building. Early in that year Holdsworth, then in London, sought the professional advice of James Gibbs, who undertook to 'revise' his plans and was paid 20 guineas by the college for his help. Lord Digby, a former member of the college who had architectural interests, was also consulted, and some sketches by Dr. Clarke suggest that he too may have had a hand in the design. The entire scheme was engraved in 1731 and was also illustrated in the University Almanack for that year.* It consisted of an arcaded quadrangle 300 feet square sited to the north of the old buildings, with a T-shaped library wing projecting from it on the west side (fig. 85). To the quadrangle the library was to present a Palladian façade based on the Queen's Gallery at Old Somerset House, and to the exterior one with a rusticated basement

* In his *Oxonia Depicta* (1732–3) Williams gives the 1731 layout, but accompanies it by different elevations (fig. 90) for the quadrangle that are inconsistent with the plan. They are not Palladian in character and their authorship is not stated.

Pl. 5. Magdalen College: a persuasive drawing from Humphry Repton's 'Red Book' of 1801. *Above*, with flap down, the view of the college from Addison's Walk as it then was, and, *below*, with flap raised, showing the Cherwell enlarged into a lake and a Gothicised Great Quadrangle open to the east.

85. Magdalen College: perspective of Edward Holdsworth's design for the Great Quadrangle and Library, as published in the *University Almanack* for 1731.

86. Magdalen College: engraved elevations of Edward Holdsworth's design, showing the west side of the Great Quadrangle, with the library in the centre (*bottom*) and the projecting west front of the library (*top*), as seen from the forecourt. The elevations are Palladian in character, the model for the lower one being the river front of Old Somerset House.

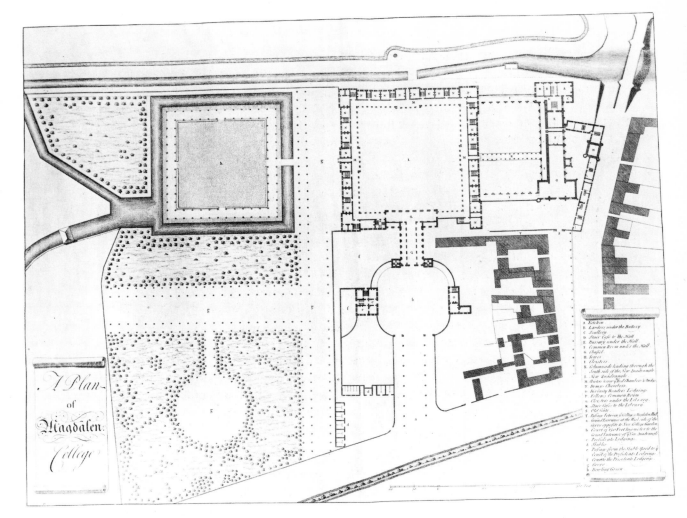

87. Magdalen College: engraved plan of the grand design by Edward Holdsworth that was adopted in 1728 (see page 81). An identical plan was published by Williams in his *Oxonia Depicta* (1732).

88. Magdalen College: Hawksmoor's revision of the plan shown in figure 87, accompanying a letter to Dr. Clarke dated 11 April 1734, in which he redraws the entrance court in the form of a circular 'Ampitheatre, and not made up of scraps, of straight lines, and crooked ones, as in the Printed Designe'. He also pleads for the retention of the Founder's Tower as 'a Treasury for Records', and shows it isolated in the Quadrangle immediately north of the chapel (Magdalen College Library).

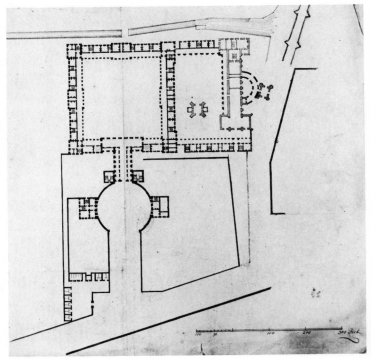

84

and twin towers in the style that William Kent was soon to make his own (fig. 86). In front of the library there was to be a curved forecourt with access to Longwall, flanked on the north by new Lodgings for the President and on the south by a smaller house for the Divinity Reader (fig. 87). This forecourt would have encroached on the territory of Magdalen Hall, and a sketch-plan exists in Holdsworth's hand showing the area that it would be necessary to purchase from the Hall.

With some modifications by William Townesend and further advice from James Gibbs, Francis Smith of Warwick and Lord Digby, the northern range of the New Building was begun in 1733 by two Oxford masons, Richard King and William Piddington. Though conforming in every essential to the engraved design, it incorporates certain improvements, of which the most prominent was the introduction of an architrave and frieze under the cornice. At each end the returns were left unfinished in preparation for the next phase of building, but few schemes as ambitious as this have been completed without modification, and the new range had hardly been completed before the layout of the quadrangle was again an open question. Already in 1734 Hawksmoor had offered some detailed criticisms of the engraved design, accompanied by drawings (figs. 88, 89), while Holdsworth continued to suggest variations on his own plan ranging from the siting of the library to the need for 'a proper place for powdering wigs in ev'ry staircase'. Writing from Rome in 1744 he sent a new plan which has not survived, and offered to furnish an elevation in which he proposed 'to borrow some hints from any of the Palaces I see in Rome. A door or a windowcase from hence may perhaps give a good air to a building'.

In the end nothing was done and the New Building stood for nearly a hundred years with its ends disfigured by the unfinished returns (fig. 91). It was not until 1791 that the scheme for the Grand Quadrangle was revived. This was the year of the election, at the age of thirty-five, of the celebrated Dr. Routh, who was to continue to preside over the college until his death in 1854, at the age of ninety-nine. It so happened that a few years previously some anxiety had been felt about the roof of the chapel, and James Wyatt was called in to advise. He rebuilt the roof, giving it a plaster Gothic vault and forming plaster niches between the windows. He was then encouraged to submit further designs for replacing the

89. Magdalen College: Hawksmoor's revision of the upper elevation shown in figure 86, accompanying a letter to Dr. Clarke dated 11 April 1734, in which he modifies the roofs so as to emphasise the corner pavilions, and alters the proportions of the towers on either side of the library, 'in much the same manner, as Mr. Inigo Jones was used to do in like case' (Magdalen College Library).

90. Magdalen College: engraved elevations of the scheme for the Great Quadrangle, published by Williams in his *Oxonia Depicta* of 1732. The upper engraving shows the façade of the library, which is based on that of Queen's College, built in 1693–6. These elevations do not agree with the plan of 1731 which they accompany in William's book, and unlike Holdsworth's published in that year (figs. 85, 86) are not Palladian in style. Their authorship is unknown, but they suggest the hand of a master-builder such as William Townesend.

91. Magdalen College: the north side of the New Building as it stood from about 1735 until the unfinished returns were faced up in 1824 (from a drawing by John Buckler in Magdalen College Library dated 1821).

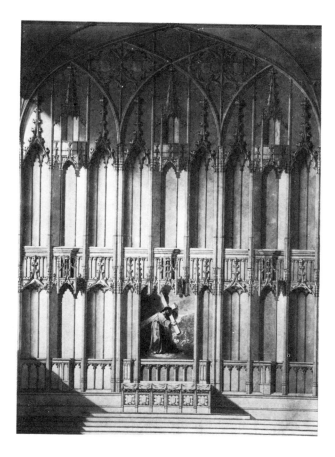

92. Magdalen College: one of James Wyatt's designs for a Gothic altarpiece in the chapel, 1791 (Magdalen College Library).

existing classical fittings and Isaac Fuller's baroque 'Last Judgement' by appropriately Gothic features. Wyatt's exquisite coloured drawings, based on authentic prototypes (including Waynflete's Chantry in Winchester Cathedral), yet as consciously romantic as a water-colour by Turner, do much to explain his growing reputation as a Gothic Revivalist (fig. 92, pl. 4). Nothing more was in fact done in the chapel, but Routh was much impressed by Wyatt's facility as a Gothic designer, and invited him to submit plans for completing the Great Quadrangle in the same style. What Wyatt proposed was to remove the north side of the Old Quadrangle and to link it to the New Building by two Gothic ranges each with a replica of the Founder's Tower in the middle. The discrepancy between the width of the Old Quadrangle and that of the New Building produced a site for a library in the re-entrant angle (fig. 93). No attempt was made to disguise the abrupt juxtaposition of Gothic and classic where the new ranges impinged on the south elevation of the New Building. The Gothic detailing was perfunctory and the total conception was as alien to the tradition of Oxford architecture as it was to the *genius loci* of Magdalen.

Later Wyatt envisaged the total demolition of the quadrangle and expressed his confidence in his ability 'to form a design that shall be perfectly consistent with the Hall, Chapel and Tower', but no drawing survives to show what he had in mind. The estimate for his original scheme was £19,000 and no money was

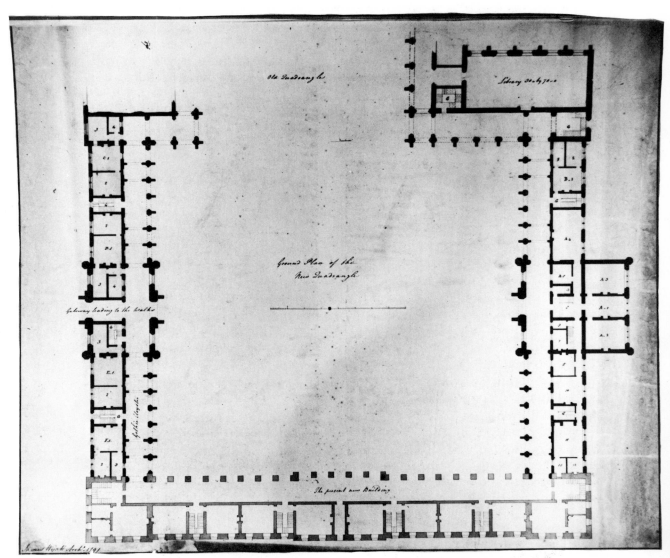

93. Magdalen College: James Wyatt's scheme for the Great Quadrangle, 1791. *Above*, a perspective view south from the New Building towards the Old Quadrangle, with the proposed new library in the re-entrant angle. *Below*, the corresponding plan (Magdalen College Library).

available after the recent expensive repairs to the roofs of the hall and chapel.

In 1796 a new aspirant came forward. This was John Buckler, clerk to R.B. Fisher, the steward of the college's estates. Buckler was a keen antiquarian draughtsman who in the course of a long life was to make more than thirteen thousand drawings of ancient buildings and who had for his time an almost unrivalled knowledge of medieval antiquities. He occasionally acted as an architect (the Gothic tablet in Magdalen Chapel to Benjamin Tate was designed by him), but never practised regularly, drawing his income from his post first as a clerk in the college's employment, and then as steward of their Bermondsey estate. Rather unexpectedly Buckler's design was classical and not Gothic (fig. 94). The New Building was to be dignified by a portico and so enabled to become the focal point of a new quadrangle. On either side a subsidiary portico would project into the quadrangle in a manner clearly suggested by Trinity College, Dublin. The north side of the old quadrangle was to be reduced to a low Gothic screen, thus linking it visually to the new Great Quadrangle without destroying its own sense of enclosure. This seems to have been a private proposal submitted by Buckler to Routh, rather than one officially commissioned by the college, and despite its considerable merits, there is no evidence that it was seriously considered.

In 1801, however, two celebrated architects were invited to submit proposals for the solution of the Great Quadrangle problem. They were John Nash and Humphry Repton, both exponents of the new picturesque approach to architecture and landscape-gardening. In recent years they had frequently worked in collaboration, but on this occasion they independently submitted different schemes.

What Nash offered was a completely new approach to the problem. So far every architect from Holdsworth onwards had ignored the park and the meadow which together give Magdalen its uniquely rural setting. The New Building, instead of helping to bring the college into relationship with the park, stood like a barrier between the two. The example of New College had been forgotten, and no one had thought in terms of an H-shaped block which might have faced the park on one side and the old quadrangle on the other without turning its back on either. It was too late now to remove the New Building, but the eastern side towards the Cherwell was still open, and Nash offered the college a series of plans which would make the most of the view over the river towards Addison's Walk. The somewhat fantastic perspective drawings illustrating Nash's scheme (figs. 95, 96) were probably the work of his French draughtsman Auguste Pugin. The lush Gothic architecture that they represent is unscholarly and meretricious (and would doubtless have been appallingly expensive to maintain), but it has the scenic quality that Nash knew so well how to exploit.

Repton's proposals were prepared in association with his son John Adey Repton, himself a pupil of Nash. Repton was, of course, primarily a landscape-gardener, but it was one of the basic principles of his approach to his art that house and garden should be brought into close association: that a park should be planned not only so as to provide picturesque prospects from the house, but also

94. Magdalen College: John Buckler's scheme for the Great Quadrangle, 1796. *Above*, looking south towards the Old Quadrangle. *Below*, looking north towards the New Building with its proposed new portico (Magdalen College Library).

95. (*facing page, above and middle*) Magdalen College: John Nash's scheme for the Great Quadrangle, 1801. A. looking west from Addison's Walk towards the detached President's Lodging, with the New Building Gothicised on the right and the north side of the Old Quadrangle dressed up to match on the left. B. the corresponding plan, with minor variations (Magdalen College Library).

96. (*facing page, below*) Magdalen College: the New Building transformed in accordance with John Nash's scheme of 1801: a view looking north, with the artist's back to the Old Quadrangle (Magdalen College Library).

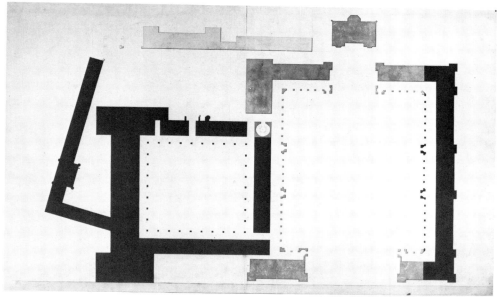

97. Magdalen College: the view of the proposed lake from the college, as presented in Repton's 'Red Book' of 1801 (Magdalen College Library).

98. Magdalen College: plan of the Great Quadrangle as proposed by Repton, with the Gothicised New Building on the left, the north side of the Old Quadrangle remodelled on the right, and the new President's Lodgings in the middle of the cross-wing (Magdalen College Library).

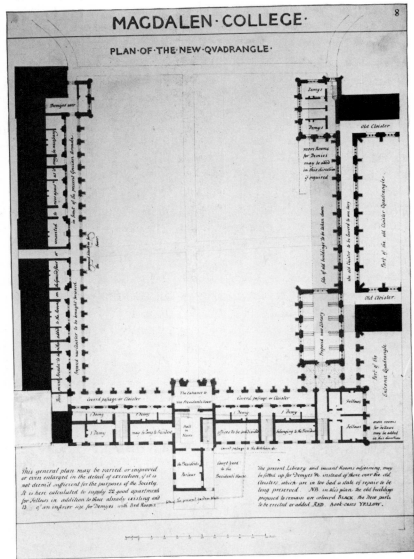

MAGDALEN · COLLEGE ·

PLAN · OF · THE · NEW · QVADRANGLE ·

picturesque views of the house from the park, and moreover that these views should change and unfold gradually as one approached, so that one got a glimpse from afar of one's architectural destination, but never saw the building as a whole until one turned the final corner. Repton in fact was a master of the art of surprise as applied to landscape-gardening. He was also a master of the art of presentation, and invariably supplied his clients with one of his famous 'Red Books' which by means of moveable flaps showed the scene both before and after improvement. Of this genre the Magdalen 'Red Book', 'finished during our Winter Residence at Bath, 1800', but not submitted until October 1801, is a particularly good example, not least in the explanatory text, in which in his usual plausible style Repton set out at once to flatter and to persuade his clients of the rightness of his ideas.

Repton, like Nash, at once saw the mistake of all previous architects in turning their backs on the park and meadow. But whereas Nash merely widened the Cherwell slightly and opened up the new quadrangle towards the east, Repton proposed to remodel the landscape itself to match his ideas for the new college buildings. Noting that the 'low, damp Meadow ... as often presents the appearance of Water, as of Land', and would therefore be difficult to 'improve' in the normal way, he proposed to convert part of it into a lake, using the excavated earth to raise the surrounding walk above flood level. At the far end a 'portico' dedicated to Addison would provide a point of vantage from which to survey the whole (fig. 97, pl. 5). The result would have been enchanting, and makes one regret that, in a city surrounded by water, Worcester is the only college with a picturesque landscape embellished by that element.

Repton then addressed himself to the great question: 'In the proposed new Buildings, what stile and character should be adopted?' Like many architects of his day, Repton was not an avowed protagonist either of Gothic or of classic, adopting either style as the occasion demanded. His principle was 'to consult the Genius of the Place'. But at Magdalen the Genius of the Place suffered from a split personality. 'Should the new Buildings', he asked, 'accord with the original date of the tower, the chapel, the hall, the cloisters &c. called Gothic? Or should they assimilate with the present New Buildings ... in the stile called Grecian Architecture?' Although by no means hostile to the New Buildings, he was decidedly of the opinion that at Magdalen the merits of the ancient buildings outweighed those of the new one, and consequently that the 'Grecian' buildings ought to be Gothicised. How this was to be done is shown in figure 98. The result would have been a Tudor Gothic group similar in character to Rickman and Hutchinson's New Court at St. John's College, Cambridge, mechanical no doubt in detail, but very effective as a backcloth to the newly landscaped grounds. As for the approaches, the ponderous old classical gateway at the end of the Gravel Walk that then led up to the west end of the chapel would be replaced by an 'open iron pallisade and gate', and an entirely new 'grand approach ... for all public or ceremonious occasions' would be formed, leading from a new gateway at the junction of Holywell and Longwall round the north side of the park and up to a new entrance contrived in the centre of the New Building (figs. 99, 100, pl. 6).

99. Magdalen College: the new gateway proposed by Repton in the middle of the Gothicised New Building (Magdalen College Library).

100. Magdalen College: view from the new gateway seen in figure 99 across the Great Quadrangle to the Old Quadrangle (Magdalen College Library).

This, as Repton pointed out, would afford just that 'effect of displaying the parts of a Gothic structure in succession and under various circumstances of perspective and relative distance' that a complex of ancient buildings like Magalen invited.

Attractive though Repton's carefully-considered proposals were, they were either too costly or too radical to be accepted. So once more nothing was done, and in 1804 John Buckler made designs for completing the New Building by adding short returns facing south at either end. In subsequent years he and his son John Chessel Buckler were employed by President Routh to provide drawings showing the effect of removing or drastically remodelling the north side of the Old Quadrangle, an idea to which the President was much attached, but which they, as antiquaries, viewed with some misgivings (figs. 101, 102). So, it seems, did the fellows, and it was decided once more to consult an architect of national repute in the person of Thomas Harrison of Chester. Although best known as a Greek Revivalist, he had rebuilt the interior of Lancaster Castle in the Gothic style, and was the architect of the very successful steeple of St. Nicholas Church in Liverpool. At Magdalen he advised that any additional buildings ought to correspond in style with the ancient part of the college, but the Gothic designs that he produced were poorly detailed (fig. 103), and his alternative proposal for a new classical building on the west side of the Great Quadrangle site was more convincing (fig. 104). At the same time the college, with characteristic inconsistency, had consulted another, much less eminent architect called Joseph Parkinson.* Parkinson at least did what Routh wanted, and declared that the north side of the cloister quadrangle was in a dangerous state. Fortified by his report, the college authorised Parkinson to carry out repairs and alterations to the Old Building that resulted in 1822 in the demolition of the whole north range with the exception of the cloister itself. Protests immediately appeared in the *Gentleman's Magazine*, then the leading organ of antiquarian opinion, and J.C. Buckler published an anonymous pamphlet violently attacking Parkinson, whose qualifications he said were merely 'good intentions and ignorance of Gothic architecture'. As for his new work, it exhibited 'errors equal in number to the bricks and blocks of stone which compose it'. A leading fellow took Buckler's side, a second opinion (critical of Parkinson) was obtained from the architect Henry Hakewill,† the President wavered, the work was stopped, and it was eventually agreed that the north side should be rebuilt on the old lines, minus the irregular but picturesque cocklofts, in a manner long since advocated by the Bucklers. As for the New Building, its two ends were finished off in a straightforward fashion in 1824 in accordance with Harrison's designs. This was the end of all the schemes for the Great Quadrangle that had been initiated just over one hundred years earlier.

The final abandonment of the Great Quadrangle in whatever form followed the

---

* Parkinson's employment is difficult to explain, but J.C. Buckler hints that it was due to 'private partiality', and it is just possible that he was related to a fellow of Magdalen called John Parkinson.

† Hakewill had remodelled the Provost's Lodgings at Oriel in 1815–17 and was in 1822 engaged in considerable works at the Middle Temple in London.

101. Magdalen College: the north side of the Old Quadrangle as it existed before 1822 (from a drawing by John Buckler in Magdalen College Library).

102. Magdalen College: drawing by John Buckler dated 1804 showing the north side of the Old Quadrangle reduced to the height of the cloister, with flanking blocks added to east and west (Magdalen College Library).

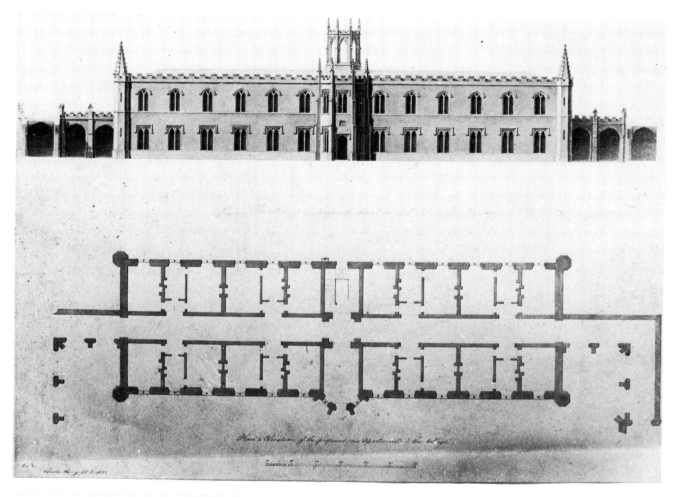

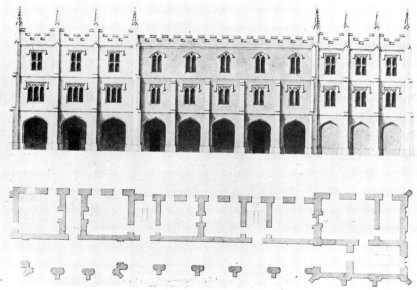

103. Magdalen College: designs by Thomas Harrison made in 1822. *Above*, for a Gothic block on the west side of the Great Quadrangle. *Below*, for remodelling the New Building in Gothic style (Magdalen College Library).

104. Magdalen College: alternative design by Thomas Harrison for a classical block on the west side of the Great Quadrangle, dated 1822 (Magdalen College Library).

acquisition by Magdalen of a new and long-coveted area for expansion. This was the site of Magdalen Hall immediately to the west of the main college buildings. Magdalen Hall had grown up as an independent university hall in part of the buildings originally intended by the college's founder, Bishop William Waynflete, for a Grammar School, and the college was anxious to regain control of buildings so close to its own. By 1820 the amalgamation of Magdalen Hall with Hertford College and its migration to Catte Street had been arranged. Simultaneously a large part of the hall's buildings were accidentally destroyed by fire. So from now on the area to the west of the old college buildings accordingly became the focus of interest for potential development. But this too presented its problems in the form of the surviving portions of Magdalen Hall, partly medieval and partly later, the adjoining President's Lodgings, Georgianised and now perceived to be out of keeping with the rest of the college, and the classical gateway, which formed the main entrance to the college from the street, and was even more repugnant to antiquarian taste.* Any new development in this area had accordingly to incorporate what was considered worth keeping of Magdalen Hall (essentially the Grammar Hall with its picturesque belfry turret, still extant), to remodel or replace the President's Lodgings, and to devise a new main entrance to the College.

But once more no decision was reached by the fellows. The remains of the Grammar Hall were repaired and made more picturesque by Parkinson, but the President continued to inhabit his simple house, with its unassuming sash-windowed front, and the offending gateway remained to affront Gothic susceptibilities. It was not for lack of projects. Harrison, Buckler and Parkinson all addressed themselves to the problem, and the college received, apparently unsolicited, an

* This gateway was built in 1635. Attributed in the nineteenth century to Inigo Jones, and in the twentieth to Nicholas Stone, it was really designed by one of the Christmas family of statuary masons – presumably either John or Mathias, since their father Gerard died in 1634. Mrs. Parry-Jones, the College archivist, has found the payment of £3. 10s. 'to Mr. Christmas for drawinge the Modell overseeinge the worke and for his twoe Journeys from London to Oxford'.

98

105. Magdalen College: anonymous design for new buildings, including a President's Lodging in the form of a Greek Doric temple, soon after 1820 (Magdalen College Library).

elaborate set of designs in the late Gothic style from a pushing young London architect called Francis Goodwin, stigmatised by J.C. Buckler as a 'bold speculator'. Although Goodwin's planning was ingenious, the fellows were not attracted by what Buckler called 'the vast and gaudy productions of Mr. Goodwin's fancy', and so his designs merely added to the mass of rejected drawings that was accumulating in the library. The anonymous author of another, apparently unsolicited design, proposed to house the President in a small Greek Doric temple and to replace Magdalen Hall by an elegant Ionic block (fig. 105).

While the need for further accommodation remained unsatisfied, the college addressed itself in 1828 to the Gothicisation of the interior of the chapel, begun by Wyatt in the 1790s, but never completed. For the first time a regular competition was held. Eighteen designs were sent in and, with the help of James Savage as assessor, those of L.N. Cottingham were accepted. Characteristically, they were not executed until the college had submitted them to yet another architect – Edward Blore – 'for his advice and consideration'. All Wyatt's work was undone, and the chapel assumed its present air of conscientious correctitude unalleviated by the slightest flight of fancy. As none of the seventeen unexecuted designs has been preserved we do not know what alternatives the college had to choose from, although a young Oxford architect, John Plowman junior, was awarded a special prize of twenty-five guineas, 'as a testimony of the credit he had done himself'. The 1840s saw the demolition of the 'Inigo Jones' gateway and the building of the Choristers' Hall (now the Library). The Hall was a competent but unremarkable performance by the younger Buckler.* But the gateway was the work of no less an architect than A.W.N. Pugin.

Pugin's employment was due to his friendship with J.R. Bloxam, a Fellow of

* For this building the College held in 1844 an abortive competition, won by J.M. Derick. But legal problems intervened and when they were resolved in 1849 Buckler's design was adopted instead of Derick's. Other architects who submitted designs in 1844 were Pugin, Allom and Scott.

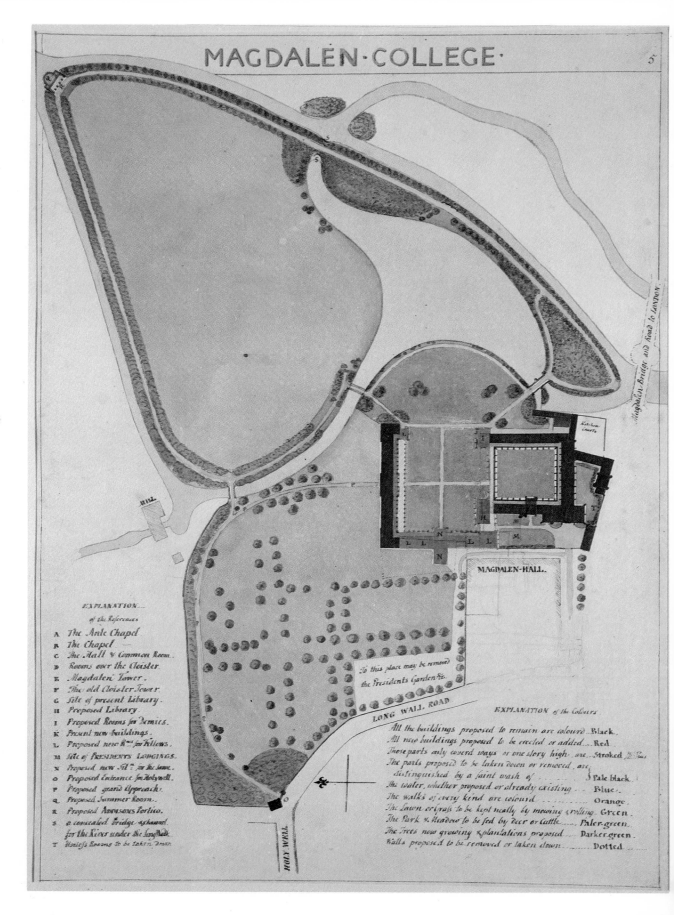

MAGDALEN·COLLEGE.

5.

MAGDALEN·HALL.

Magdalen Bridge and Road to London.

Kitchen courts

MAGDALEN·HALL.

To this place may be removed
the Presidents Garden &c.

LONG WALL ROAD

HOLY WELL.

HILL.

EXPLANATION
of the References

A The Ante Chapel
B The Chapel
C The Hall & Common Room
D Rooms over the Cloister
E Magdalen Tower
F The old Cloister Tower
G Site of present Library
H Proposed Library
I Proposed Rooms for Demies
K Present new buildings
L Proposed new R{ms} for Fellows
M Site of Presidents Lodgings
N Proposed new R{ms} for the same
O Proposed Entrance from Holywell
P Proposed grand Approach
Q Proposed Summer Room
R Proposed Ambrosons Portico
S a concealed Bridge & channel
   for the River under the Long Walk
T Useless Rooms to be taken down

EXPLANATION of the Colours

All the buildings proposed to remain are coloured ... Black.
All new buildings proposed to be erected or added ... Red.
Those parts only coverd ways or one story high are ... Stroked with lines
The parts proposed to be taken down or removed are
  distinguished by a faint wash of .... } Pale black
The water, whether proposed or already existing ... Blue.
The walks of every kind are coloured .... Orange.
The Lawn or grass to be kept neatly by mowing & rolling. Green.
The Park & Meadow to be fed by deer or Cattle ... Paler green.
The Trees now growing & plantations proposed ... Darker green.
Walls proposed to be removed or taken down ... Dotted.

High Church leanings whose rooms at Magdalen were the meeting place of all those interested in the early stages of the Oxford Movement. With Pugin's aid they were decorated with a triptych of the Adoration and other ecclesiological furniture, and on the table there stood a model in wax of Bishop Waynflete's tomb in Winchester Cathedral.

Pugin had made measured drawings of Magdalen, a college which he regarded as 'one of the most splendid and perfect collegiate edifices remaining', and he and Bloxam both deplored the existence of 'the Italian Barrack in the park'. This was immoveable, but the gateway, already in bad repair and admired by nobody, was an easier victim, and President Routh was sympathetic. At a time when the sight of a cross on an altar could arouse a feeling of 'indescribable horror' in the mind of a Protestant clergyman, the erection of a gateway prominently surmounted (as in Pugin's design) by this symbol of Popery was bound to cause some disquiet, but Bloxam carried the day, and at the end of the year 1844 he had the satisfaction, in his capacity as Vice-President, of making (in Latin) the following entry in the College Register:

> At the beginning of this year the President and the majority of the Fellows, with few dissentients, determined that the great or outer gateway of the College, built in 1635, and, like other works of that century, extremely hideous, should be destroyed. The new one, in a style conforming to the adjoining buildings, was entrusted to Augustus Welby Northmore Pugin, easily the leading architect of the present time, who, having begun it in the month of August, has since brought it to a happy conclusion. The expenditure on the gateway amounted to £679 os. 7d.

The gateway (figs. 107, 108) was Pugin's only executed work in Oxford, and a minor one at that. But coming so soon after the rejection of his designs for Balliol and the erection of the memorial to the Protestant Martyrs, it was something of an architectural manifesto, and it is a pity that the building of the new St. Swithin's Quadrangle in the 1880s should have entailed its demolition.

The persistent failure to enlarge Magdalen during the first half of the nineteenth century meant that by 1875 one third of the college's junior members had to be accommodated outside its precincts. At last, in 1879, the Governing Body determined to act. Magdalen Hall was the designated site, and four well-known architects were invited to compete: G. F. Bodley and his partner T. Garner, Basil Champneys, G. E. Street and W. Wilkinson. Bodley, Street and Wilkinson were all established Gothic Revivalists, though Wilkinson was better known for his domestic architecture in North Oxford than for any university work, and Street's architectural allegiance was to the thirteenth rather than to the fifteenth century in which Magdalen's existing buildings were constructed. Champneys was a younger man who had some Gothic work to his credit and would soon have more, but at Cambridge he had just designed Newnham College in the red brick style of Norman Shaw. At Magdalen all four architects took it for granted that their aim should be (in Champneys' words) 'to follow as closely as possible the spirit of the

101

Pl. 6. (*facing page*) Magdalen College: plan showing Humphry Repton's proposed improvements, including a lake associated with Addison's Walk, a Gothicised Great Quadrangle (shown in red), and a new 'Grand Approach' from Holywell round the edge of the deer-park (Magdalen College Library).

106. Magdalen College: design for St. Swithin's Quadrangle by Basil Champneys, 1879 (*Building News*, 1 July 1881).

107. Magdalen College: design for St. Swithin's Quadrangle by G. E. Street, 1879. Pugin's gateway is on the right. (Magdalen College Library).

108. (*facing page*, *above*) Magdalen College: design for St. Swithin's Quadrangle by William Wilkinson, 1879. Pugin's gateway is in the centre, opposite the west end of the chapel. (Magdalen College Library).

109. (*facing page*, *below*) Magdalen College: design for St. Swithin's Quadrangle by Bodley and Garner, 1879. This was the winning design, but only two of the three sides of the quadrangle were built, the north (right-hand) wing being omitted. Pugin's gateway is on the extreme left. (Magdalen College Library).

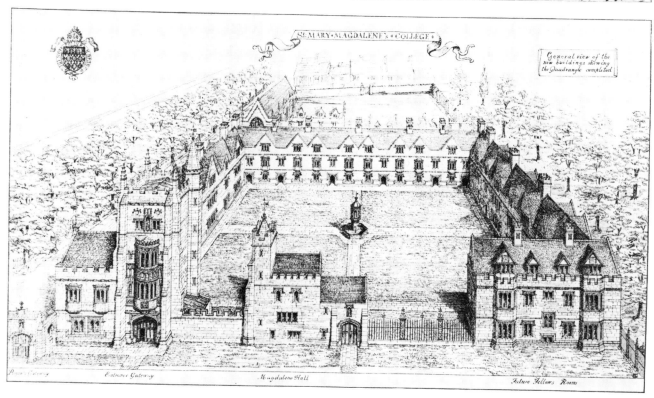

ST·MARY·MAGDALEN'S·COLLEGE

General view of the
new buildings shewing
the Quadrangle completed

Entrance Gateway   Magdalene Hall   Future Fellows Rooms

ancient buildings'. 'This is not', declared Bodley and Garner, 'a place for the display of much originality of design, or for the importation of any foreign treatment of architecture. The Gothic should be that not only of earlier Oxford, but that of Magdalen.' Given these aspirations, Bodley and Garner had all the scholarship and expertise necessary to achieve them, and they duly gained the commission. The building proposed by Champneys was punctuated by three towers, one at each end of the High Street front, and a third in the middle (fig. 106); it would somewhat have exceeded its allotted space, encroaching at the eastern end on the approach to the President's Lodgings. Street envisaged only one tower, but his walls were enlivened by corbelled projections, chimneys and variegated fenestration to a degree that looks fussy (fig. 107). Wilkinson submitted a very competent gabled elevation with tall staircase windows of the sort used by Deane in the Meadow Buildings at Christ Church (fig. 108). His gatehouse, moreover, really fulfils that function, whereas Bodley and Garner's stands forlornly at one end of their principal range, pointlessly echoing the Founder's Tower opposite (fig. 109).

Only the south and west sides of Bodley and Garner's three-sided quadrangle were actually built (in 1880-4), and when Sir Giles Scott was invited to extend their building in 1928 he did not follow their plan, but added a new leg running first north and then westwards to Longwall, where a small gateway gives access to the street. For this gateway Scott made an alternative design in deliquescent Gothic which remains in the College archives. Thus ended Magdalen's long involvement with the Gothic Revival, more productive of abortive designs than of executed buildings, and far from outstandingly successful even in those that were carried out.

How is this epic of architectural mismanagement to be explained? Much of the blame must be given to President Routh, an elderly and eccentric recluse who, while himself dabbling in architectural improvement, failed for fifty years to give a decisive lead, and indeed proved to be 'painfully timid' in architectural debate, and apt to 'recoil before even a feeble opposition'. Though architects were only too willing to come forward with plans, they do not appear ever to have been given a proper brief, and at a time when the architectural profession was still in a formative stage, they were unconstrained by any of those standards of conduct which would, at a later date, have helped to guide them in their relations with an exceptionally capricious corporate client. So Magdalen drifted from one architect to another, gradually accumulating that anthology of unexecuted designs upon which this chapter is based. When, in 1879, a century's indecision was at last resolved, a properly conducted competition produced some highly professional designs, but the failure to complete Bodley and Garner's quadrangle in the form they had envisaged threw away the opportunity to create a new academic precinct and left the St. Swithin's Building literally 'out on a limb'. Thus Magdalen today consists of a medieval nucleus with two incomplete additions, one of the eighteenth and the other of the nineteenth century. The result is a collection of buildings that, despite the quality of their architecture and the beauty of their setting, still lacks the essential unity of a college.

VII

Pugin and the Battle for Balliol

MUCH MORE MOMENTOUS than Pugin's minor conquest at Magdalen was his defeat at Balliol. Pugin's involvement with Balliol was due indirectly to J. R. Bloxam, his friend and patron at Magdalen, who introduced him to W. G. Ward, a Fellow of Balliol who, like Bloxam himself, was an ardent High Churchman. Visitors to Ward's rooms found his tables ostentatiously covered with the folios of St. Thomas Aquinas and St. Bonaventura. Architecturally speaking, however, he was as yet uneducated. 'What an extraordinary thing', Pugin remarked to Bloxam, 'that so glorious a man as Ward should be living in a room without mullions to the windows.' He was even more astonished to discover that Ward did not know what a mullion was. Ward was not long allowed to remain in ignorance of this cardinal point of architectural orthodoxy, and the outcome was a plot to get Pugin, Catholic though he was, accepted as the architect of a new, Gothic, Balliol – a Balliol that should be a manifesto of architectural High Churchmanship in a university then preoccupied with religious controversy.

Something certainly needed doing at Balliol. There had of course been some new building there in the past. First the Bristol Building overlooking St. Mary Magdalen's churchyard had been put up by the Townesends in 1716-20, then the south-east corner of the old college had been rebuilt, also by Townesend, in 1738-43 (figs. 110-11). Henry Keene's Fisher Building followed in 1768-9, and finally another block had been added on the Magdalen Street front in 1825-6 to the designs of George Basevi. But the old quadrangle was in a bad state. Already in 1791 James Wyatt had found the roofs in a dangerous condition and strengthened them. He also made designs for rebuilding the street front in a nominally Gothic style with large square-headed windows and a battlemented parapet (fig. 112). The result would have been very similar to the exactly contemporary Holmes Building at St. John's, in which Wyatt may well have had a hand, as it was built by his henchman James Pears. Then in 1843 Basevi had advised the complete rebuilding of the front to Broad Street. He proposed to remove the Master's Lodgings to St. Giles' in order to provide more rooms in Broad Street, and submitted designs 'in a plain but handsome manner' to cost £10,000. These designs were placed in the library for inspection by the fellows and others so that 'opinion may be collected from Persons of Taste and skill in Architecture'.

110. Balliol College: anonymous scheme illustrated in the *Almanack* for 1742, and partly executed in 1738–43 (Ashmolean Museum).

111. Balliol College: the Broad Street front in about 1860, showing the partial execution of the scheme shown in figure 110 (Oxfordshire County Libraries).

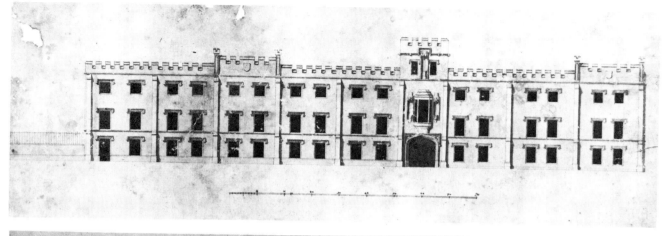

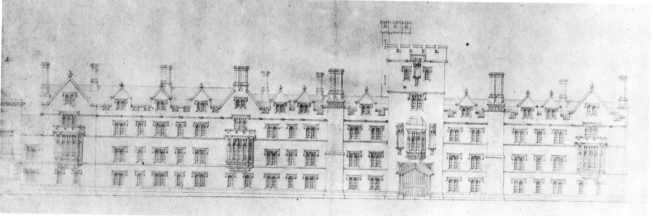

112. Balliol College: design for rebuilding the Broad Street front by James Wyatt, 1791 (Balliol College Library).

113. Balliol College: design for rebuilding the Broad Street front by George Basevi, 1843 (Balliol College Library).

Opinion was on the whole adverse, 'it being thought that ... Mr. Basevi had been guided more by the elegance and symmetry of Grecian and Italian models, than by the irregular grandeur of Gothic architecture'.

As figure 113 shows, Basevi's elevation, though by no means out of keeping with the Oxford collegiate tradition, was open to the same criticism as Barry's designs for the Houses of Parliament, of which Pugin himself had remarked: 'All Grecian, Sir: Tudor details on a classic body.' Windows were large in proportion to the wall-area, and arranged in a manner that was too obviously derived from Georgian fenestration. Although they had the support of the Master, Dr. Richard Jenkyns, Basevi's plans were rejected as 'inadequate to the general notion and expectation of such a building as ought to form the front of the College towards the Broad Street'. Basevi, hurt and dispirited, retired from the scene, complaining of amateurs who did not hesitate to pass judgement on matters about which they were not qualified to form an opinion. 'We do not', as his brother put it, 'read that

107

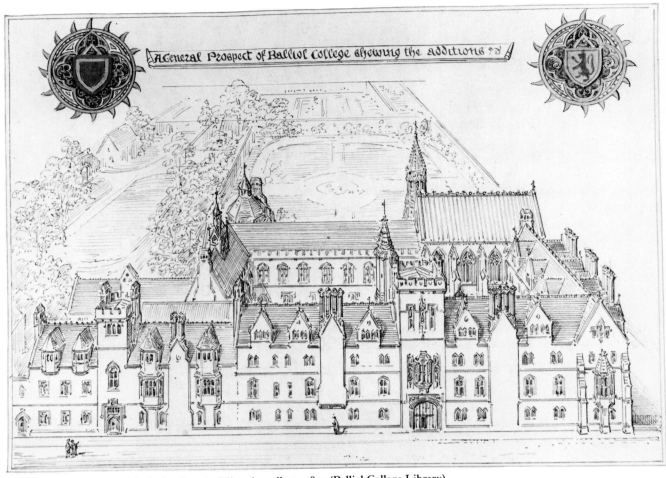

114. Balliol College: Pugin's design for rebuilding the college, 1843 (Balliol College Library).

Pericles invaded the functions of Phidias.' But in Balliol in 1843 an analogy from ancient Greece cut little ice: for Ward and his ally Oakeley (then the Senior Fellow) were all out to secure the employment of Pugin, whose architectural battle-cry was that 'a man who paganises in the Universities deserves no quarter'.

When he saw Basevi's drawings Pugin did not hesitate to condemn them as 'utterly destitute in the true and ancient spirit of design – they might be for anything . . . a Blind Asylum or a Missionary College. For even *they* build Gothic now.' As for removing the Master's Lodgings to a new site, that was wrong in principle. 'When the Abbots ceased to reside with their communities and built separate lodgings, the rule and spirit was fast going to decay. And I believe the same remark is applicable to collegiate discipline.' Here we are far from straightforward aesthetic criticism, far even from serious consideration of collegiate planning. Here we have the spirit of Pugin's *Contrasts* applied to Oxford – the present weighed in the balance against the past and found wanting, the advocacy of Gothic as a style morally superior to classic, and the planning of a college as the

108

first step in a crusade to put the clock back to an idealised medieval past in which dons taught Catholic doctrine in rooms with oriel windows and undergraduates slept in canopied beds with prie-dieu by their side and improving texts round their walls (figs. 114-18).

Pugin's missionary zeal, his passionate identification of architecture with moral values and moral values with the Catholic faith, proved his undoing. Only three years earlier he had violently denounced the Martyrs' Memorial which had just then been built round the corner in St. Giles'. The Reformers were 'vile, blasphemous imposters pretending inspiration while setting forth false doctrine', while the subscribers to the Memorial were 'foul revilers, tyrants, usurpers, extortioners and liars'. What is more, they had found, in Gilbert Scott, an architect who was almost as clever as Pugin himself in interpreting the Gothic style in a genuinely medieval manner. If the Protestants were going to steal his style, then he would infiltrate himself into an Anglican college and transform it into the semblance of the Catholic college it once had been, and might, with the aid of the two Tractarian Fellows, be once more. So Pugin's invitation to submit designs for Balliol was part of a battle, not merely of styles, but of religious politics. Gothic might be the right style for the new Balliol, and Pugin might be the best interpreter of that style, but to employ him would be a victory for the Romanists, a slap in the face for all who wanted to preserve the Established Church as it was, for all who believed in the cause for which the Protestant martyrs had died.

Dr. Jenkyns, the Master, was decidedly one of these, and he was not prepared to have Pugin officially recognised as Balliol's architect. When, therefore, on 6 March 1843, it was agreed 'that Mr. Pugin be requested to furnish a design for a new façade towards the Broad Street', it was at the same time resolved 'that under the peculiar circumstances of the case, even if Mr. Pugin's plan should eventually be approved and be thought worthy of being carried into effect, he himself be not employed in the execution of the work'.

This, as Pugin told Bloxam, would amount to a kind of architectural suicide. Nevertheless he agreed to the terms and after two weeks of manic work produced, singlehanded, the necessary drawings. There was one set of plans, elevations and sections for the Governing Body and another of perspectives, bound up like a missal, with gilt clasps and illuminated title-page (pl. 7), to seduce those whose hearts yearned for the lost enchantments of the Middle Ages. What Pugin's drawings disclosed was a Balliol transformed by that combination of scholarship and fantasy which was his speciality. The front to Broad Street had as its centrepiece the old fifteenth-century entrance-tower. This tower was of the standard Oxford type with three niches, the two lower of which Pugin proposed to fill with 'images' of the Founder, John de Balliol, and the Lady Devorgilla his wife. On either side mullioned and transomed windows with ogival heads alternated with boldly expressed chimney-stacks. To the left the Master's Lodging was distinguished by a secondary tower and two oriel windows. The roofs throughout were to be high pitched and surmounted by a 'stone cresting artificially wrought with Lions, Katharine Wheels, and the words "I. Balliol. Devorgilla" in

115. Balliol College: Pugin's design for the interior of the kitchen, 1843 (Balliol College Library).

116. Balliol College: Pugin's design for the kitchen, 1843 (Balliol College Library).

pierced metal'. Inside the quadrangle the old hall and library were to be retained and restored, but there was to be a new chapel in the style of the fourteenth century (fig. 117) and a prominent new kitchen with a pyramidal roof – based on the one at Stanton Harcourt rather than on the Abbot's Kitchen at Glastonbury (figs. 115–16).

It was, however, in the interior that Pugin's genius as a Gothic Revivalist was most clearly in evidence, from the Master's library with its linenfold desk and candle-lit lectern to the chapel with its floor of 'incrusted tiles', its oak roof 'painted azure with stars and swans of gold', its organ carved with 'angels playing on instruments' and its 'crockets, finials, bosses, strings, corbels, canopies etc.... busy in entail and of diverse designs'.

It was a brilliant performance and Pugin calculated that it would set the fellows 'half mad for true Christian Rooms'. What it actually did was to start a controversy so violent that the Master subsequently, with the consent of the fellows, thought it prudent to remove from the College Register the record of one of the most heated debates in the history of Balliol. What was said on that occasion we shall never know, but a week later Jenkyns summoned the fellows to a special meeting in the chapel, at which he made, with the greatest formality, the following declaration:

110

117. Balliol College: Pugin's design for the interior of the chapel, 1843 (Balliol College Library).

118. Balliol College: Pugin's design for an undergraduate's bedroom, 1843 (Balliol College Library).

After a careful consideration of the language and spirit of our Statutes, and under a strong sense of the obligation imposed on the Master by the terms of the oath taken at his admission, I am compelled to declare that I can neither sanction the employment of Mr. Pugin as an Architect, nor consent to an agreement for carrying into effect by him, or any other Party, any plan which he may furnish for repairing or rebuilding that part of the College in which the house, of right belonging to me, is situate.

By refusing to allow his house to be rebuilt Jenkyns effectively vetoed the whole scheme, and by the solemnity of the declaration he gave it the force of a sentence of excommunication. Pugin was banished from Balliol, but a majority of the fellows was still determined not to accept a design by any other architect, and on 4 April at a stormy meeting all plans for rebuilding were set aside indefinitely; it was agreed merely to repair the roofs of the south front. Nothing more was done until after Jenkyns' death in 1854, when it was decided to rebuild the chapel as a memorial to him and William Butterfield was employed to design a building as redolent in its way as Pugin's of the High Churchmanship which Jenkyns had so resolutely opposed.

Meanwhile Pugin's designs remained in the College Library, and when in 1866

119. Balliol College: the Broad Street front as built to the designs of Alfred Waterhouse in 1867-8 (from a Victorian photograph in the library of the Oxfordshire Architectural and Historical Society).

the generosity of Miss Brackenbury permitted the college to think once more of rebuilding the front quadrangle, they were lent to Alfred Waterhouse, and undoubtedly influenced the building which we see today in Broad Street, though its detailing is a century earlier in character than Pugin's (fig. 119). By then architectural style and religious belief were no longer so closely identified with one another. Even Nonconformists were worshipping in Gothic chapels, and no one doubted that Gothic was the proper style for an Oxford college, nor that in designing it the architect should be as faithful to medieval forms as he desired. And so it fell to the Quaker Waterhouse in some measure to realise the vision of the Catholic Pugin and to give to Broad Street that carefully calculated irregularity, that show of corbelled-out oriels and crested gables, that twenty years earlier had seemed to be the very symbols of heresy within.

*　　　*　　　*

Architecturally, the most conspicuous results of the Tractarian movement in Oxford were Keble College, Exeter College Chapel, and the Churches of St.

112

Philip and St. James, and St. Barnabas. But almost every parish church or pre-Reformation college chapel was 'restored' in accordance with High Church principles, and even a Low Church college like St. John's felt impelled to sweep away the existing interior of its chapel (which included a screen designed by Sir Christopher Wren) in favour of a new Gothic ensemble, refraining only from the richly coloured garnishings which went with Tractarian worship. The chapel, as remodelled by Edward Blore in 1843, has a hammer-beam roof. An alternative design by Blore for a plaster vault is illustrated in figure 120.

A much more striking manifestation of architecture as the handmaid of religion is afforded by the Holy Trinity Convent in the Woodstock Road. In 1864 this community of Anglican nuns, temporarily established in St. John Street, decided to move to a new site at the junction of Woodstock and Bevington Roads, and Charles Buckeridge, a pupil of Scott's then practising in Oxford, was appointed architect. His first design (fig. 121) was an embodiment in stone of the concept of the Trinity to which the community was dedicated. The triangular plan was a development of a diagrammatic representation of the Trinity common in medieval iconography (fig. 122). In this a central circle represents 'God', while three subsidiary circles symbolise 'Father', 'Son', and 'Holy Ghost'. The inscrutable paradox of the relationship between the Persons of the Trinity is emphasised by linking ligatures inscribed 'is' and 'is not'. Taking this figure as the basis of his design, Buckeridge worked out a plan in the form of a spherical triangle (a geometrical form often found in medieval window tracery), with a trilobed chapel

120. St. John's College: alternative design for remodelling the interior of the chapel by Edward Blore, 1843 (St. John's College muniments).

113

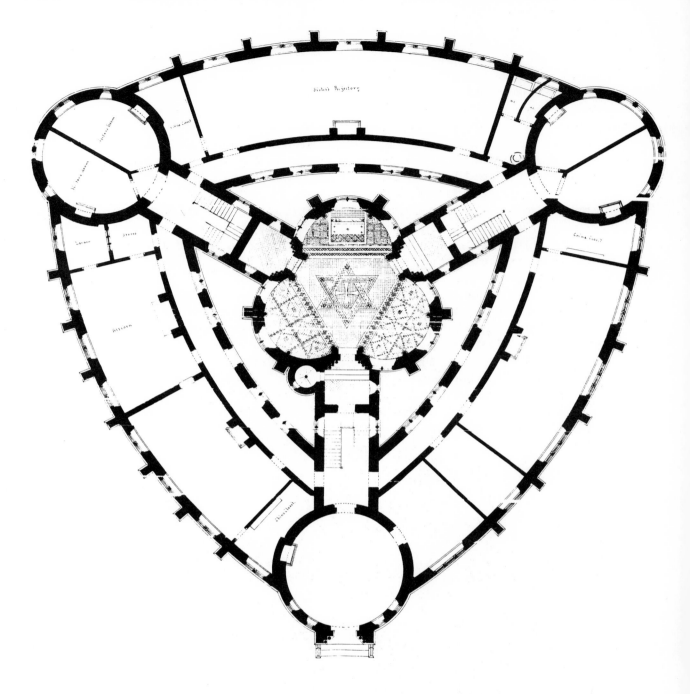

121. Holy Trinity Convent: unexecuted design by Edward Buckeridge symbolising the Holy Trinity, 1864 (St. Antony's College Library).

122. The Holy Trinity as diagrammatically represented in medieval manuscripts.

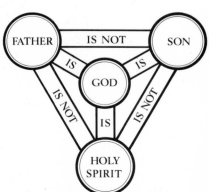

114

123. Holy Trinity Convent: detail of Buckeridge's design showing the central chapel with its pyramidal roof and spire (St. Antony's College Library).

in the centre, linked by staircases to circular rooms marking the three corners of the building. Internal cloister walks provided access to the principal rooms, which were arranged on three floors. All the necessary conventual accommodation was more or less satisfactorily fitted into this plan. The one surviving elevation shows the roof of the chapel, crowned by a tall *flèche*, rising above the surrounding buildings, which are thirteenth-century Gothic in style (fig. 123). In the end the Trinitarian design was abandoned for reasons either of impracticability or of expense, and the existing more conventional building (now St. Antony's College) was built instead in the years 1866–8.

VIII

The Two Museums

FROM THE early nineteenth century onwards the architectural history of Oxford is strewn with rejected plans. For by then a competition had become one of the established ways of choosing an architect. The first regular architectural competition open to all was for the bridge over the Thames at Blackfriars in London in 1759-60, and thereafter competitions became increasingly common. They were very rarely resorted to by private individuals, whose selection of an architect would be based on personal taste or private recommendation, but for a board or a committee or a corporate body such as a university a competition provided a choice of designs for discussion, and it was chiefly to serve the great explosion of public and corporate building in the late eighteenth and early nineteenth centuries that the competition developed. It also reflected the rapid growth in the architectural profession itself, and the greater mobility afforded by improved transport, both of which made it possible for an architectural competition to attract entries from all over the country. Although the conduct of such competitions often left much to be desired from the point of view of the competitors, they were by the 1820s and 1830s a fact of British architectural life which only the most well-established of architects could ignore.

At Cambridge in 1804-6 a major controversy over the design of Downing College had resolved itself into an irregular competition which established William Wilkins' architectural ascendancy in that university. In 1822, 1829 and 1834 there were important competitions, conducted with varying degrees of propriety, for King's College, the University Library and the Fitzwilliam Museum, and less important ones for the Observatory in 1821 and the Pitt Press in 1828. In Oxford during the same period the only major competitions were for the County Hall (1837) and what is now the Ashmolean Museum (1839), but there were several minor ones, e.g. for the church at Carfax (1819), the interior of Magdalen College Chapel (1828) and the enlargement of the Market (1839).

The irregular way in which architectural competitions were often conducted in the early nineteenth century is illustrated by the case of St. Martin's Church at Carfax. By 1819 it had become apparent that the old medieval church was past repair and would have to be rebuilt. In view of the long and close connection between the Corporation and the church, the City Council voted £600 towards the cost, and a committee was appointed that included, besides the rector and churchwardens, the Mayor, the Provost of Oriel and other leading citizens. In announcing a competition the committee emphasised that it hoped that 'the elevation and exterior decoration of the Building may prove a distinguished ornament to the City, and form a termination worthy of one of the finest streets in Europe'. The result, in the estimation of most people, fell far short of this ambition, and there is all too much reason to suppose that it was (as the Vice-Chancellor put it) 'quite a made up job'.

How many designs were submitted is not recorded, but the competitors included the Quaker Thomas Rickman, then just entering on his career as a Gothic Revival architect, the London architect J.B. Papworth, and the Oxford architect-builders Daniel Harris and John Plowman, working in partnership. Papworth was adjudged to have won the competition, and duly received the premium of £30 offered for the best design, but the committee nevertheless announced that it had given the commission to the two local men. This decision, perverse though it sounds, was nevertheless compatible with the conventions normally governing architectural competitions, which did not bind the organisers to accept the winning design. But according to Papworth the plan adopted was not the one originally submitted by Harris and Plowman, and fairly judged in competition, but 'a fresh design', produced subsequently and very likely improved in the light of the other competitors' proposals. Papworth's drawings survive in the R.I.B.A. Collection (fig. 124). Although of a kind that would have been anathema to the

124. St. Martin's Church at Carfax: design submitted by J. B. Papworth in the competition of 1819 (R.I.B.A. Drawings Collection).

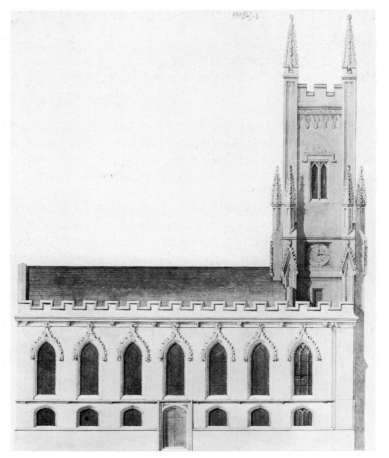

118

125. St. Martin's Church, Carfax, as built to the designs of Daniel Harris and John Plowman in 1820-22 (National Monuments Record).

Gothic Revivalists of the next generation, his design had a touch of theatricality that might have endeared it to present-day taste. As it was, Plowman's rather perfunctorily Gothicised stone box (fig. 125) was certainly no great ornament to the city, and its demolition in 1896 in order to widen the street need cause no serious regret.

The Shire Hall competition of 1837 appears to have been better conducted, for although the successful architect was once more a local man in the person of John Plowman junior (son of Harris's partner), he was both the author of the winning design and the architect appointed to carry it out. Again little is known about the designs submitted by the unsuccessful competitors, except that some were 'Grecian' and others 'Gothic' or 'Norman' in character. No guidance as to style was given in the directions to competitors, the Justices of the Peace merely requiring 'a substantial Edifice, with Stone Exterior, encumbered by no Ornament, but at the same time bearing a handsome and characteristic appearance'. However the *Oxford Times* expressed the view that a Grecian design would not be appropriate

119

126. The Shire Hall, as built to the designs of John Plowman, junior, in 1839-41.

127. The Martyrs' Memorial: design published by Edward Tatham in 1777. It was intended to stand in Broad Street.

'either for the site or for accordance with adjacent buildings, and that the Gothic or Norman would be preferable styles; but more particularly the latter', and by selecting Plowman's 'Norman' design the Justices showed that they were of like mind. In similar situations other counties (e.g. Cumberland, Lincoln and Norfolk) had opted for Gothic, but at Oxford the proximity of the eleventh-century castle mound and St. George's Tower was evidently felt to demand round arches and roll mouldings. Though Plowman's elementary essay in Romanesque, its entrance guarded by fasces formed of cast-iron battle-axes, is difficult to take seriously, it is interesting as one more instance of that deference to the past that has been so characteristic a feature of Oxford's architecture (fig. 126).

The years 1839 and 1840 saw two further competitions, for the Ashmolean Museum and the Martyrs' Memorial, respectively. The idea of a memorial to the Protestant bishops burned at the stake in Broad Street in 1555-6 had been suggested as long ago as 1773 by Edward Tatham, later Rector of Lincoln, in a pamphlet* full of ideas for architectural and environmental improvement, some perverse (like the demolition of the cloisters at New College in order to reveal the west end of the chapel), some enlightened (such as the formation of a square at

* *Oxonia Explicata et Ornata*, of which there were further editions in 1777 and 1820. Tatham's own design for the Memorial is illustrated in the 1777 edition. It was to consist of a light classical archway, surmounted by a figure of Victory, and flanked by statues of the two bishops (fig. 127), and was intended to stand in Broad Street.

120

Carfax), and some prophetic (notably the cutting of a new street from St. Giles' to Worcester College, accomplished in the 1820s). Tatham's suggestion lay dormant until 1840, when it was revived under the influence of religious controversy. What he had envisaged as an elegant embellishment to Broad Street became (on a different site at the bottom of St. Giles') a manifesto of anti-Tractarian feeling. A committee was formed, money was subscribed and in March 1840 a limited competition was organised. The promoters were, however, so specific about what they wanted (a restored and enlarged version of the Eleanor Cross at Waltham) as to give little scope for invention on the part of the competitors. Given the terms of the competition Gilbert Scott's carefully detailed version of the Waltham Cross can hardly be faulted, and it is certainly better proportioned than the one submitted by J.M. Derick (the runner-up), whose original drawing survives in the Bodleian (fig. 128). Scott himself thought, not unjustifiably, that his cross 'was better than any one but Pugin would have produced'.

It was, however, the competitions for the two museums that were to be the

128. The Martyrs' Memorial: *left*, design submitted by J. M. Derick (Bodleian Library, MS. Top. Gen. a.4, f.8), *right*, the Memorial as built to the design of Sir Gilbert Scott (from a Victorian photograph).

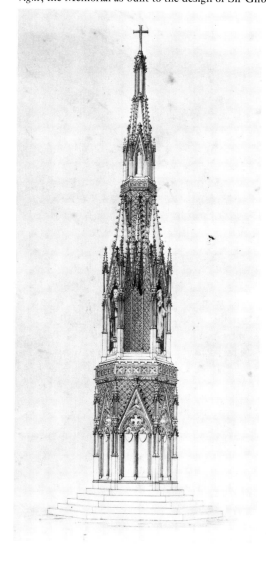

great architectural events of early Victorian Oxford. On 10 June 1839 the Registrar announced that the University intended to erect a new building on the corner of St. Giles' and Beaumont Street in order to house the University Galleries and the Taylorian Institute. New galleries were needed to contain the classical sculpture and other works of art displaced from the Schools Quadrangle in order to make way for books, while the Taylorian Institute was designed to give effect to the will of the architect Sir Robert Taylor, who had left money for the study of modern languages in Oxford. The decision to unite two buildings with quite different functions on the same site was an odd one, but the instructions to competitors were explicit that while the two institutions were to be 'entirely distinct in their internal arrangements', they should nevertheless 'harmonize, and, if possible, form parts of one architectural design, which is required to be of a Grecian character'.

'Grecian' in contemporary parlance meant 'neo-classical' in general rather than 'Greek Revival' in particular. But the stylistic stipulation was hardly necessary, for in 1839 it would have been generally accepted in architectural as well as academic circles that a building designed to house an important collection of sculpture and other works of art would be in a classical style. All the great purpose-built museums of Europe – the Museo Pio-Clementino in the Vatican, the Munich Glyptothek, the Altes Museum at Berlin, and the British Museum in London, were neo-classical buildings, and it was most unlikely that in 1839 Oxford University would countenance any deviation from this stylistic convention. However one Gothic design (of a totally impracticable character) had been submitted in the recent competition for the Fitzwilliam Museum at Cambridge, and it may have been thought advisable explicitly to exclude anything of the sort from the Oxford contest.

By the closing date of 19 October 1839 twenty-seven sets of designs had been sent in. Relatively few of the competitors were architects of the first rank, perhaps because (as Dr. David Watkin has suggested) the Gothic Revival was already beginning to attract the more enterprising young architects, and it was young architects above all who entered for public competitions. Out of the twenty-seven competitors, only three were architects of national standing: C.R. Cockerell, T.L. Donaldson and Anthony Salvin. Of these Donaldson was shortly to become Professor of Architecture at University College, London, where he was responsible for the very handsome library, while Salvin was to make his name as a Gothic Revivalist, but had designed a handful of minor country houses in a plain classical manner. Cockerell was by far the most distinguished of the three both as a scholar and as a practising architect: he was, moreover, at the height of his career, and had already had important commissions in Cambridge, London and Edinburgh. Cockerell and Salvin both figured in the short list which the committee of Delegates drew up in November, the other names being those of Messrs. Mair and Browne, John Plowman (the architect of the Shire Hall), and Henry Hakewill. Sir Robert Smirke (the architect of the British Museum) was then asked for his observations on these selected plans. Cockerell's he pronounced to be 'an excellent

122

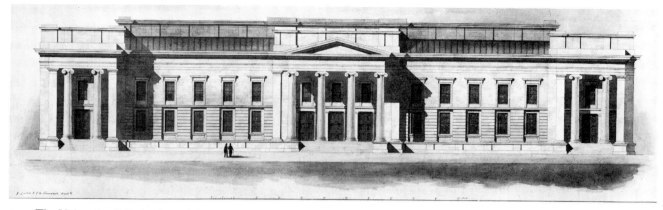

129. The University Galleries (now Ashmolean Museum) and Taylorian Institute: competition design by G. Gutch and E. W. Trendall, 1839 (Bodleian Library, MS. Top. Gen. a.9).

example of that style of Grecian Architecture which is seen in the best works of Italian architects of about the sixteenth century'; Mair's and Browne's he described as 'Grecian architecture of suitable and dignified character', but pointed out that their plan exceeded the limits of the site by several feet in both directions; Plowman's he dismissed as having 'the character of a distinguished residence rather than a collegiate [i.e. academic] Establishment', Hakewill's as 'not possessing any striking character of design in the exterior', while Salvin's he could not fully make out, 'being covered with a uniform dark tint which obscures the details'.

Aided by Smirke's assessment, the Delegates recommended, and Convocation agreed, to give the first prize to Cockerell and the second to Plowman. It is unfortunate for the student of unbuilt Oxford that only one of the rejected designs is known to survive (fig. 129). It was submitted jointly by George Gutch and E. W. Trendall. It shows a routine Greek Revival design very similar in character (and equal in dulness) to Smirke's own General Post Office in London, and serves only to show how infinitely more complex and subtle was Cockerell's winning design, in which Antique, Renaissance and even some Baroque elements are fused into a composition of outstanding distinction.

The design accepted in 1839 underwent considerable modifications in detail before the building was brought to completion in 1845. Of these (discussed in detail by Dr. Watkin in his biography of Cockerell) the most important were the substitution for the conventional Ionic and Composite orders shown in the original drawings (cf. fig. 130) of the order of the Temple of Apollo at Bassae with its more vigorously curving volutes (fig. 132), and alterations to the relationship between the round-headed windows and the attic storey into which they penetrate in a manner of which Hawksmoor would certainly have approved. In the interiors there is less evidence of change in Cockerell's ideas, as he had probably not worked out the arrangements in much detail in the competition drawings. Happily in both parts of the building they remain very much as he left them, the only serious loss being the hemicycle containing statues of the Nine Muses, destroyed in 1893 to make way for what is now the Oriental Gallery, which is illustrated here (fig. 131) as something that, although actually built, is so little known that it might never have existed.

130. (*top*) The University Galleries (now Ashmolean Museum) and Taylorian Institute: the winning design by C. R. Cockerell, showing features subsequently modified in execution (*Oxford University, City and County Herald*, 19 June 1841).

131. (*above*) The University Galleries (now Ashmolean Museum): the hemicycle facing the main entrance, destroyed in 1893 (Bodleian Library, MS. Top. Oxon. b.89, f.12).

132. (*right*) The University Galleries (now Ashmolean Museum) and Taylorian Institute, showing details of the Ionic order as executed.

124

The building of the University Galleries and Taylorian Institute excited no controversy. Most of the money was provided by private benefaction, and Cockerell's reputation as a scholar must have done much to recommend his design to members of Convocation: indeed the approbation of the University was speedily demonstrated by the conferment of an Honorary Degree upon the architect. It was to be otherwise with the University Museum.

The idea of a University Museum formed part of a campaign to persuade a conservative university to make Natural Science a normal part of its curriculum. The leaders of this movement were H.W. Acland, the Professor of Clinical Medicine, and David Williams, Warden of New College. They were supported, not merely by medical and scientific colleagues, but by influential churchmen, some of whom (including Bishop Wilberforce) recognised that Nature was the work of God, and its study therefore an eminently Christian activity, while others (such as Dr. Pusey) were, like the scientists, challenging an established order that was equally hostile to change whether theological or scientific. The battle for an Honour School in Natural Science was won in 1850, and the next step was to obtain a building in which the sciences could be studied and taught with the aid of medical, chemical, geological and zoological collections properly arranged and displayed. What was envisaged was therefore much more than just a museum – it was what would nowadays be called a Centre for Scientific Studies, and it was to provide lecture-rooms, laboratories, dissecting-rooms and a library, besides a large area for the exhibition of scientific specimens.

It so happened that at this time the University had in hand a sum of nearly £60,000 derived from the profits of the Clarendon Press, and Acland and his supporters hoped to secure some of it for their Museum. In January 1851 a proposal in Convocation to allot £53,000 to the erection of examination schools, lecture rooms and a museum was rejected. However in 1852 the Museum Committee received support from the University Commissioners, who recommended that the University 'should proceed with the plan for building a Museum for all departments of physical science'. At last, in 1853, a site in the south-west corner of the Parks was purchased from Merton College, and in April 1854 Delegates were appointed to obtain designs for a building to be erected there. They announced a competition, with prizes of £150, £100 and £50. 'No limitations as to the style of architecture' were to be imposed, 'but architects should bear in mind that excellence of interior arrangement will be judged more essential than exterior decoration'. The general layout of the building was indeed specified: it was to consist of a large central court, roofed with glass, to contain the collections, and surrounded on three sides by lecture-rooms and laboratories. With the aid of an architect called Rohde Hawkins (son of the keeper of antiquities at the British Museum), the Delegates had satisfied themselves that such a building could be erected for £30,000, and no design was to be considered whose estimated cost exceeded that amount. By December thirty-three designs had been received and were exhibited in the Bodleian gallery. The *Builder*, which devoted several columns to the competition, analysed them as follows:—

Gothic of all kinds	12
Greek, more or less German in treatment	3
Roman, more or less after Wren, with pedimented porticos, columns, &c.	4
Italian, more or less Barryan or Palatial	6
Elizabethan	1
The Order of Confusion	2
Original, Crystal Palace work tacked on to various regular book details	3
Abominations, about	2

In the *Builder's* opinion the medieval designs were 'by no means the best', the styles selected being 'rather ecclesiastical than collegiate', and more German than English. The Grecian designs, however, were banal, and the *Builder* reserved its praise for a drawing bearing the motto *Spes*, which 'presents us with a really noble arrangement of a great circular hall, domed and lit after the fashion of the Pantheon at Rome', and for another labelled *Fiat Justitia* which, behind a classical façade in the style of Barry's Treasury Buildings in Whitehall, offered two alternative interiors, one ('A') 'a fine glass vault, extending longitudinally, with contributory glass vaults running into it at a low level, somewhat after the manner of the Basilica of Constantine at Rome', the other ('D') 'a noble hall leading immediately into a long glass-vaulted nave, the end of which terminates in a glass dome, from which depart right and left two similar vaulted naves – the three naves forming altogether a T shape'. The author of *Fiat Justitia* was in fact Charles Barry's younger son E. M. Barry, and drawings of the exterior and of version 'A' of the interior are preserved in the R.I.B.A. Collection and in the Ashmolean Museum. Behind a rich classical façade with a long Corinthian portico *in antis* Barry offered a museum in the form of a great architectural glass-house – a mini Crystal Palace inside a many-columned temple from Palmyra or Baalbek (figs. 133-4). The author of *Spes* is not known, but from the *Builder's* description it sounds as if he could have been William Hosking, Professor of Architecture at King's College, London, who in 1849 had submitted a Pantheon-like scheme for a British Museum reading-room.

The Delegates themselves short-listed six designs which they categorised as follows:—

'A–Z'	Italian
'Cross Compasses'	Jacobean
'Fiat Justitia'	Palladian
'Nisi Dominus'	Rhenish Gothic
'Spes'	Roman
'Virtus'	Belgian Gothic

'A-Z' and *Fiat*, they said, 'present a long and rather low and uniform front. *Spes* a large columniated mass. *Virtus* the air of a Belgian Hotel de Ville with points resembling the Tuileries palace. 'Cross Compasses' and *Nisi* a more varied and more aspiring outline'.

126

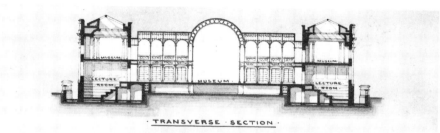

· TRANSVERSE · SECTION ·

· LONGITUDINAL · SECTION ·

PLAN OF GROUND FLOOR

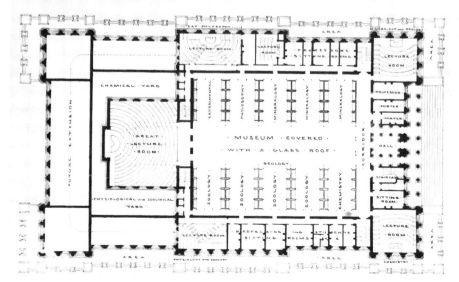

These six designs were submitted to the well-known London architects Philip and P.C. Hardwick, who were asked to say whether they could be executed for the specified sum of £30,000 and to pronounce on the soundness of the construction in each case. When the answer came that 'not one' of them could be built for that amount, the Delegates concluded that as the competitors had all failed to conform to this important limitation, they were not bound to award any prizes. Should they 'convey a moral lesson to architects' by adhering strictly to the terms of the competition, or offer *ex gratia* 'awards' instead of prizes? In the end they decided to be generous.* Meanwhile, they recommended Convocation to choose between *Fiat Justitia* (by E.M. Barry) and *Nisi Dominus* (by Deane and Woodward of Dublin). On 11 December 1854 Convocation decided in favour of *Nisi Dominus* by a large majority (eighty-one to thirty-eight).

The choice of a Gothic design for the Museum was an event of some importance in English architectural history. Gothic churches, country houses and collegiate buildings there were in plenty. But since the Houses of Parliament there had been no major public building in the Gothic style, and certainly no museum. What is more, the Oxford Museum was no conventional product of the Gothic Revival, but one designed by a brilliant young Irishman named Benjamin Woodward (his partner Sir Thomas Deane managed the business side of the practice). Woodward equalled Pugin in his flair for re-creating medieval architectural forms, and surpassed him in his capacity for realising them in three dimensions. He was, moreover, attuned to the ideas of John Ruskin, who was a close friend of Acland. The adoption of features from continental Gothic was something Ruskin had been advocating for some time, and in the University Museum the prominent crested roofs, the diapered slating and the use of different-coloured stones were all foreign (mainly Flemish and North Italian) features of the sort he was endeavouring to introduce into the vocabulary of the English Gothic Revivalists. In fact, as Acland was later to recall, 'the actual designs attracted much attention, more even than the contest whether modern Science should find a worthy dwelling-place in Oxford'.

This double victory - of Science over obscurantism, and of Gothic over classic - was not easily won. There were not wanting those who, like J.W. Burgon, a Fellow of Oriel and one of the Delegates, regarded Deane and Woodward's design as 'strange, bizarre and detestable', or who shared Tennyson's opinion that it was 'perfectly indecent'. There were those who thought it inappropriate to use Gothic for so secular a purpose, and those to whom it seemed almost sacrilegious to spend on a Science Museum money earned by printing Bibles. There must have been many who, even if they accepted that Science must have its place in Oxford's curriculum, found the self-conscious medievalism of its architectural setting incongruous. 'Nothing', wrote Fergusson in his *History of the Modern Styles of Architecture*, published in 1862, 'was to betray the hated and hateful nineteenth

---

*E.M. Barry received £100, and Francis Mangnall ('A-Z') and John Thomas ('Cross Compasses') got £50 each.

century, to the cultivation of whose sciences [the Museum] was to be dedicated
... The lecture-rooms are cold, draughty, and difficult to speak in. The library is
a long ill-proportioned gallery, with a rudely constructed roof, painted in the
crudest and most inharmonious colours ... and the bookcases arranged, not to
accommodate books, but to look monkish. You take a book from its press, and are
astonished to find that men who could spend thousands on thousands in this great
forgery have not reprinted Lyell's *Geology* or Darwin's *Origin of Species*, in black
letter, and illuminated them, like the building, in the style of the thirteenth
century ... On wandering further you enter what seems a kitchen of the age of
that at Glastonbury, and find a professor, not practising alchemy, but repeating
certain experiments you believe to be of modern invention ...' The detached
laboratory (fig. 135) was, indeed, one of the more extraordinary conceits of the
Gothic Revival – nothing less than a carefully-detailed version, complete with

135. The University Museum, as built to
the designs of Deane and Woodward, 1855–
60. The 'Abbot's Kitchen' is on the right
(*The Builder*, 9 April 1859, p.253).

129

pyramidal roof and tall chimney-stacks, of a medieval kitchen such as the well-known 'Abbot's Kitchen' at Glastonbury. Inside the main building the problem of finding appropriate medieval forms for modern needs was even more manifest: for the iron girders that support the glass roof (fig. 136) are bent into the form of acutely-pointed Gothic arches in a manner that belies their true nature, and betrays the principle of truth in architectural design to which Ruskin and his followers were dedicated.

How was it that this bizarre and illogical building, a kind of scientific Strawberry Hill, should have been accepted first by the scientists themselves and then by the whole university? A glance at Barry's rival design, coarsely and conventionally detailed in the overblown classical style of the 1850s, emphasises the freshness and originality of Deane and Woodward's Gothic vision, jejune though it might be. But their triumph was not merely an aesthetic one. The propagandists of Gothic architecture had been at work, insisting that it was as right for secular buildings as it was for ecclesiastical ones (a point easily appreciated by those who had purchased Hudson Turner's book on the *Domestic Architecture of the Middle Ages in England*, recently published by J.H. Parker and on sale in his shop in Broad Street), and emphasising that it was far more adaptable than the classical alternative. There was, declared Sir Gilbert Scott, 'no purpose under the sun, to which the principles of Gothic architecture ... do not admit of being adapted'. G.E. Street, the architect to the diocese of Oxford, published a pamphlet in which he not only stressed this point, but offered a sketch for a Gothic museum with a tower somewhat like that of Jacques Cœur's well-known house at Bourges and with crocketted gabling over the windows reminiscent of the fourteenth-century town hall at Brunswick (fig. 137). J.H. Parker followed suit with a pamphlet stressing that English Gothic architecture too could 'be made subservient to

136. (*facing page*) The University Museum: iron girders in the interior masquerading as Gothic arches (*The Builder*, 23 June 1860, p.399).

137. The University Museum: 'Sketch for a Museum' by G. E. Street, to illustrate his *Plea for the Revival of True Principles of Architecture in the Public Buildings of Oxford* (1853).

almost any plan without in the least degree destroying its character'. Indeed there was some force in these contentions. As M. J. Johnson, the university astronomer or 'Radcliffe Observer', put it at one of the Delegates' meetings, the activities for which the Museum was to cater were diverse and their respective collections were not susceptible of symmetrical arrangement. So 'that kind of architecture was to be preferred, which did not recognise symmetry as one of its essential conditions'. The great advantage of Gothic, he said, was that it 'admitted of irregular development'. The truth of Johnson's argument became apparent in 1868-9, when the new Clarendon Laboratory (designed by T.N. Deane) took the form of a separate but related block such as Barry's strictly symmetrical and self-sufficient building would never have tolerated within its curtilage. Of this greater flexibility the detached laboratory itself was a good example, for its purpose was to keep the fumes of chemistry (like the smells of cookery) well away from the main building. Even the high entrance tower might (according to Johnson) be useful in providing ventilation, 'especially if the Professor of Chemistry were to ... entertain an audience by making stinks', as a visiting German professor had done 'in a manner of which Dr. Daubeny, no doubt, entertained as lively a recollection as he did'.

Gothic also scored in the important matter of cost. Only two-thirds of Barry's building could be executed for the money available, whereas of the six short-listed designs Deane and Woodward's was the one that least exceeded the stipulated limit. In fact, with the omission for the time being of most of the sculpture, it was understood that it could just be built for the £30,000 voted by Convocation (though in the end it cost a great deal more).

Finally, in trying to understand why Deane and Woodward's foreign-looking Gothic should have been regarded as more suitable for the purposes of nineteenth-century science than Barry's grand parade of Roman columns, we may wonder whether it was partly because the orders were, after all, so closely associated with the dead hand of classical learning from which the scientists were seeking to liberate themselves. It was certainly in some degree because Gothic was a style in which Nature was supposed to find expression in a way that the established conventions of classical architecture could hardly permit. If one compares a regular Corinthian capital of the sort intended by Barry (fig. 139) with one of those in the courtyard of the Museum (fig. 138), systematically arranged to represent 'various groups of plants and animals, illustrating different climates and various epochs', one can see how Gothic satisfied the Ruskinian principle that 'all art should be informative, conveying truthful statements about natural facts', whereas Barry's conventionalised acanthus did not. Now these were the sort of sentiments that, as Acland wrote, 'animate the earnest student of Gothic'. Earnestness was, above all, what the Gothic Revivalists had in common with the Victorian scientists, whereas the advocates of a classical design were at best scholars, arguing about esoteric refinements, or at worst the dull practitioners of an enervated style that by the 1850s had exhausted every expedient in its repertoire from Ancient Greece to Renaissance Italy. In a classical building like the Ashmolean Museum one might have a fine display of archaeological erudition sensi-

Pl. 7. Balliol College: the frontispiece of Pugin's book of designs, submitted to the College in 1843, and conceived in the form of a medieval illuminated manuscript. The founder and foundress John de Balliol and his wife Devorgilla kneel on either side of a miniature drawing of Pugin's design. The inscription and the date 1843 are carefully written in medieval characters (Balliol College Library).

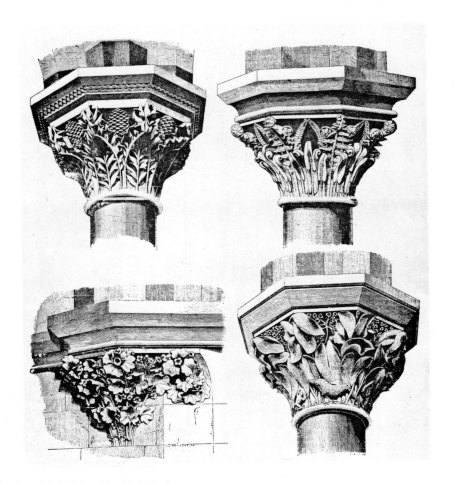

138. The University Museum: capitals and a corbel
carved naturalistically to represent cycads, ferns, mallow
and water plantain (*The Builder*, 18 June 1859, p.408).

139. A conventional Corinthian capital.

tively adapted to modern purposes, but only in a Gothic one like the Museum of
Science could one have a series of marble columns each different, and each with
its own geological message directed at the impressionable mind of the serious
undergraduate. In the last resort, indeed, it was the moral and symbolical superiority of Gothic that won the day. For these were attributes of the style calculated
to appeal to clergymen like Dr. Pusey and his Tractarian followers, and on 11
December 1854 it was their votes that gave *Nisi Dominus* its decisive majority over
Fiat Justitia.

134

IX

Jackson and the Jacobean Revival

DURING THE last quarter of the nineteenth century Oxford's favourite architect was T.G. Jackson (1835-1924). Jackson was trained in the office of Sir Gilbert Scott, but like several of his fellow-pupils, renounced Gothic orthodoxy in favour of a more eclectic historicism. Whereas Bodley and Garner simply moved on chronologically from 'Geometrical' to 'Decorated', and J.J. Stevenson to a vernacular domestic style akin to that of Norman Shaw, Jackson emerged as a neo-Mannerist for whom English Jacobean Architecture, French and Italian Renaissance detailing, and even the rich internal decoration of the period of Wren, were all legitimate sources of inspiration, to be used separately or in conjunction as fancy or circumstance might suggest. Gothic might still be suitable for churches, but (as Jackson argued in a book called *Modern Gothic Architecture* which he published in 1873) it was no longer appropriate for the mass of nineteenth-century building. The four or five hundred years that had elapsed since the Middle Ages had not (as the Gothic Revivalists maintained) all been an architectural disaster: on the contrary they offered much to the modern architect whose eyes were not closed by Gothic dogma: 'this consideration suggests to us the advisability, nay more, the necessity of a judicious eclecticism'.

Jackson's 'judicious eclecticism' is to be seen all over Oxford – at Corpus, Hertford, Lincoln, Somerville, Trinity, at the former Boys' and Girls' High Schools and above all at the Examination Schools. Look at the High Street front of the Schools and you are looking at a façade derived from an English country house of the late sixteenth century (Kirby Hall, in fact), with the oriel window of its great hall duplicated at either end. Go round the corner and you see an open-ended quadrangle with a frontispiece of superimposed orders in the Oxford tradition, but with pedimented windows at the end of each wing that recall some East Anglian country house such as Heydon or Honingham. Go inside and you find yourself standing on a mosaic pavement of Roman character, looking up at an open roof of the English hammer-beam type and at a stone gallery supported on Italianate Renaissance arches. Nearby there is a staircase, exquisitely made of coloured marbles like an ambo or a pulpit in San Clemente in Rome or San Miniato at Florence. Upstairs and downstairs, inside the examination rooms, there are panelled doors and pedimented chimney-pieces such as one finds in

English domestic architecture of what Jackson's generation called 'the later Renaissance', i.e. the period of Wren. It is all beautifully done, with a virtuosity (though not a fertility of invention) almost equal to that of William Burges, and it stands as a monument to the prestige and importance of the Oxford examination system as established by the reforms of the nineteenth century.

Jackson's great weakness lay not so much in his artistic promiscuity (fully apparent only to the professional architect or architectural historian) as in not knowing where to stop. He would repeat a motif *seriatim* where it would have been more effective in isolation, or try simultaneously to express two architectural ideas in a situation where there was room for only one. Of the former failing the High Street front of Brasenose is a prime example (fig. 162). Here seven highly ornamented oriel windows compete for attention in a façade where a medieval architect (or a nineteenth-century one like Pugin who was more sensitive to medieval precedent, cf. fig. 114) would have introduced only one to dignify the Principal's Lodgings at one end and a second (not necessarily identical) to balance it at the other. Both failings are exemplified at Hertford College, where Jackson uses three 'Palladian' windows in a façade where established English usage would have been satisfied with one flanked by two openings of simpler character, and where, instead of being content with introducing this triple central feature between the existing late Georgian wings, he cannot refrain from inserting two intrusive bay windows as well. Here, as elsewhere, he protested (in architectural terms) too much.

How far these criticisms occurred to Jackson's Oxford patrons I do not know. No doubt his exuberance appealed to late Victorian taste and, if his ornament was often redundant, its elegant detailing invariably saved it from vulgarity. But in Oxford Jackson enjoyed a unique advantage: alone among professional architects before or since, he was a Fellow of a College and a Senior Member of the University.

Jackson's academic career (an open Scholarship, a second in Classical Moderations and a Third in Greats) was not very distinguished, but his Scholarship made him eligible (under the statutes then in force) to compete for a non-resident fellowship at Wadham, which he gained in 1864. This fellowship was all-important for Jackson's career, for at a time when he was barely earning his living as an architect, it enabled him to travel and it was his travels in France and Italy that opened his eyes to the merits of styles other than the fourteenth-century Gothic to which Scott's office was dedicated. Jackson's fellowship also brought him his first architectural commission in Oxford in the form of alterations to the Warden's Lodgings at his own college (1872).

It was (Jackson tells us) 'in consequence of' this work at Wadham that in 1874 he was invited to compete for the completion of the bell-tower at Christ Church. This tower, enclosing the great staircase that leads up to the hall, was incomplete at the time of Wolsey's fall and had remained so ever since. Until 1870 its upper part formed an inoffensive extension of the hall, whose balustrade (added in the seventeenth century) it shared. But in 1870 Scott, in the course of restoring the

136

Cathedral, ejected the bells from the central tower (which he wanted to open up above the crossing) and hung them over the staircase tower in an unsightly timber-framed erection ridiculed by C.L. Dodgson as 'a tintinnabulatory tea-chest'. The only way of getting rid of this excrescence was to heighten the tower so as to form a proper belfry, and in 1873 the Governing Body of Christ Church appointed a committee to obtain designs. By now Scott's credit was running low at the House, and the committee proposed to invite several architects to compete. Scott was informed that it was hoped that he would not 'object to be included' in their number. After a struggle his ambition overcame his self-esteem and at the last moment he agreed to submit designs. The other architects on the committee's list were A.W. Blomfield, William Burges, Basil Champneys, T.N. Deane, J.W. Hugall,* G.E. Street and Alfred Waterhouse. Of these only Champneys, Deane and Hugall accepted, so the Belfry Committee decided to approach G.F. Bodley, T.G. Jackson, J.L. Pearson, Anthony Salvin and Henry Woodyer. Bodley and Jackson accepted, and in due course the members of the committee had before them eleven designs, one each from Champneys, Deane, Jackson and Hugall, two from Bodley and no fewer than five from Scott.

In the minutes of the committee (kept by Vere Bayne) the principal designs are described as follows:—

Bodley:	'a leaden Bell structure with 4 Turrets at the corners' and an alternative which 'makes the Tower into a College Gateway, and leaden Pepperbox on top'.
Champneys:	'the top is like a Mayday Garland'.
Deane:	an 'Italian Campanile'.
Jackson:	a 'Grand Tower 170 feet high'.
Hugall:	——
Scott:	two 'different stone square towers', one 'octagon, lead and wood much ornamented', a 'taller octagon, same style, two stories', and one 'square, lead and wood'.

Of these, Bodley's first design, a picturesque Gothic lantern with Tudor detailing (fig. 140), Deane's 'campanile', Jackson's 'grand tower' (fig. 141) and one of Scott's square stone towers (fig. 142) were considered possible. When two sessions of voting (recorded in detail) resulted only in the elimination of Scott, leaving no clear preference as between Bodley, Jackson and Deane, the decision had to be left to the Governing Body of the college. Here conflicting motions ('to adopt Mr. Jackson's Tower', 'to take Mr. Bodley's Gateway as a basis', 'to ask Mr. Bodley for a fresh design, wholly in stone', etc.) resulted in no absolute majority. Straight votes between different pairs of architects indicated a general preference for Bodley, but it was finally agreed (by nineteen votes to six) 'to get Bodley and

* The inclusion of the relatively obscure Hugall (d. 1878) must have been due to the fact that at the time he was altering or rebuilding two Berkshire churches in the patronage of Christ Church: Easthampstead and Eastgarston.

PROPOSED NEW BELL TOWER
CHRIST CHURCH OXFORD

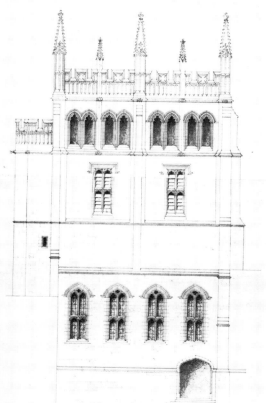

140. (*facing page*) Christ Church: design for the bell-tower by G. F. Bodley, accepted in 1873 and partially executed (Christ Church archives).

141. Christ Church: rejected design for the bell-tower by T. G. Jackson, 1873 (Christ Church archives).

142. Christ Church: rejected design for the bell-tower by Sir Gilbert Scott, 1873 (Bodleian Library, MS. Dep. a. 17/4).

Deane to work together if possible in preparing a design', and if not possible to give the commission to Bodley alone. As there can have been little real hope of finding any common ground between Bodley's Gothic fantasy and Deane's 'Italian campanile', Bodley was left in possession of the field, though almost every detail of the design (which included the battlements and pinnacles of the hall) had to be thrashed out with a committee by no means disposed to defer to his judgement on any single point.

So far as the belfry was concerned the Governing Body proceeded step by step, authorising the building of the stone tower before it had made up its mind about the lantern, and when the stonework was nearly complete it merely directed the architect to finish it off with a roof of sufficient strength 'so as not to reject the idea of hereafter putting up the Lantern'. A decision about the latter was in effect postponed *sine die*. The result was a massive rectangular tower whose large corner pinnacles but relatively small intermediate ones, well calculated as satellites to the proposed lantern, are scarcely adequate to serve as its principal vertical features (fig. 143). What was intended merely as a substructure sits ponderously in the south-east corner of Tom Quadrangle, a monument to the vacillation of a Governing Body that, having chosen a grand design, did not have the courage to carry it through. If a lantern was not wanted, then Scott's modest and well-proportioned belfry would clearly have been a better choice.

As for Jackson's soaring tower it was a spectacular essay in late Perpendicular architecture, but as an addition to Christ Church it was of questionable merit. Offset at one corner of Tom Quadrangle, it would have related awkwardly to the college as a whole and to the cathedral spire in particular. It was (so Jackson was told) because it put the latter out of countenance that the Dean for one was against it. But Jackson's defeat was an honourable one. His design was illustrated in the *Architect* and two members of the Governing Body admired it so much that they bought the original drawings and gave them to the Senior Common Room.

143. Christ Church: the belfry as built without the lantern (cf. fig. 140).

The building that established Jackson's reputation in Oxford was the Examination Schools in the High Street. The need for new examination schools arose partly from continued pressure from the Bodleian to take over the existing rooms in the Schools Quadrangle in order to house books, and partly from the inadequacy of those rooms to accommodate the increasing number of candidates presenting themselves for examination. For some time the Sheldonian Theatre, the Old Ashmolean Museum and the Clarendon Building had been annually pressed into service as overflow examination rooms, but the inconvenience of supervising candidates in more than one place was considerable, and an entirely new building was the obvious answer.

In 1869 a committee was appointed by the Hebdomadal Council (the governing body of the University) to take steps to remedy the situation, and a site was obtained on the south side of the High Street. The committee then addressed itself to the choice of an architect. Each of its eight or nine members 'named two architects; and the number of names was then reduced by successive votings, until the ultimate choice fell upon Mr. Street and Mr. Deane'. G.E. Street was by now one of the leading Gothic Revivalists and the architect of Cuddesdon College and of St. Philip and St. James's Church in North Oxford. T.N. Deane was the son and successor of Sir Thomas Deane, the co-architect of the University Museum, and had recently designed the Meadow Building at Christ Church.* Deane's plan was the one preferred, but before it could be put before Convocation some adjoining property became available and the architect was asked to submit revised plans taking advantage of the enlarged site.

When in November 1870 members of Convocation were invited to approve Deane's designs they found two alternative schemes displayed for their inspection. One was distinguished by a large entrance hall, 'intended to give shelter in bad weather to men waiting for the opening of the Schools', beyond which the examination rooms were arranged on either side of a 'wide and well-lit corridor'. In the other Deane substituted for the 'Waiting Hall' an entrance tower and vestibule, leading to a cloister surrounding a courtyard seventy feet square. Deane himself strongly advocated his second scheme, but on 6 December 1870 both were rejected by Convocation. If the rejected design was anything like the fussy and overcrowded one that Deane submitted two years later (fig. 145) the decision was understandable.

In 1872 Council tried again. A new committee or 'Delegacy' was appointed, and Blomfield, Deane, J.O. Scott, Street and Waterhouse were invited to engage in a limited competition. Street and Waterhouse declined, and of the three designs submitted, the Delegates recommended those of John Oldrid Scott, Sir Gilbert Scott's second son. Some of Scott's drawings survive, and what they show is a

---

* In 1859 Deane and his partner Benjamin Woodward had made an extraordinary design for remodelling the front of Christ Church with a high-pitched roof and gabled windows in the style of a French Gothic château (fig. 144). The object seems to have been to obtain additional accommodation, and this was eventually achieved in a different manner by the erection in 1863 of the Meadow Building to the designs of Deane alone, Woodward having died in 1861.

144. Christ Church: design by Deane and Woodward for re-modelling the front of the college with a high-pitched roof and dormer windows in the French château style (the Irish Architectural Archive, Dublin).

145. The Examination Schools: design by T. N. Deane rejected in 1873 (*The Architect*, 2 August 1873).

142

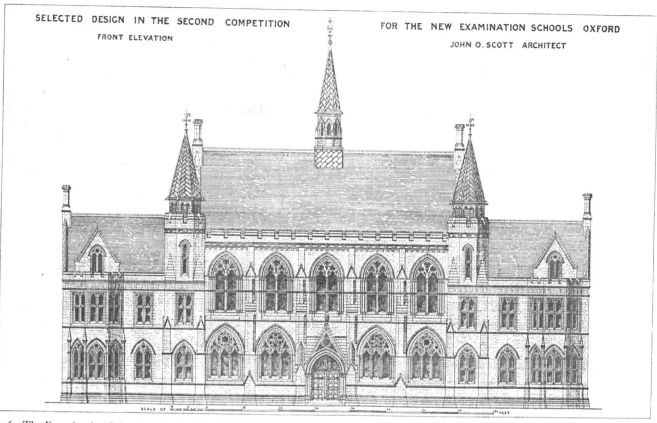

SELECTED DESIGN IN THE SECOND COMPETITION   FOR THE NEW EXAMINATION SCHOOLS OXFORD

FRONT ELEVATION   JOHN O. SCOTT ARCHITECT

146. The Examination Schools: early Gothic design by J. O. Scott rejected in 1873 (*Building News*, 1 Oct. 1875).

building in a thirteenth-century style with features derived (according to Scott) from the Bishop's Palace at Wells. There was to be a vaulted entrance hall and the examination rooms were arranged round a cloister. To the High Street the building would have presented a façade of five bays surmounted by a high pitched roof and flanked by a pair of turrets rising out of lower wings (fig. 146). After a good deal of criticism, both of the turrets (on the ground that they were purely ornamental, containing no staircases) and of the plan (which grouped the tall buildings round an unduly small quadrangle) Scott's plan was rejected on 27 May 1873 by fifty-four votes to twenty.

In 1875 yet another Delegacy set to work to try to produce an acceptable plan. In a desperate attempt to get the much-needed Schools built, its members were authorised to separate the entrance hall from what lay behind, and to procure plans and estimates for the two sections separately, 'in the hope that possibly a plan for well-arranged Schools might be adopted, even if architectural opinion be against the plan proposed for the front Hall'. The Delegates proceeded to draw up a list of possible competitiors which at first included nearly every eminent Victorian architect, but eventually resolved itself into a short list of five – E.M. Barry, G.F. Bodley, T.N. Deane, R. Norman Shaw and J.O. Scott, and a reserve list consisting of T.G. Jackson, Basil Champneys, A.W. Blomfield and Philip Webb. Barry and Norman Shaw having declined, Jackson and Champneys were brought in to compete with Bodley, Deane and Scott.

143

147. The Examination Schools: late Gothic design by J. O. Scott rejected in 1875-6 (*Building News*, 1 Sept. 1876).

With the exception of Jackson's, all the designs submitted were Gothic. Bodley's were in the late Gothic collegiate style that he understood so well, while Scott, sensing that enthusiasm for thirteenth-century Gothic was on the wane, produced an elaborate essay in Tudor Gothic arranged round a cloistered courtyard (fig. 147). Champneys, too, offered a nicely detailed though rather awkwardly planned scheme in the 'English third-pointed style' which (as he said) was 'thoroughly characteristic of Oxford' (fig. 149). But it was Jackson's bold amalgam of English Elizabethan and Jacobean architecture with French and Italian decorative forms that won the votes first of the Delegates and then of Convocation. The University's readiness to forsake its faith in Gothic as the only acceptable alternative to Greek or Roman, combined with Jackson's freedom from stylistic restraints, enabled him to provide relatively comfortable rooms for the conduct of examinations instead of his rivals' Gothic halls. His Examination Schools were like a great Elizabethan mansion that had been gradually adapted to the taste of later times, while theirs necessarily maintained something of the inconvenience of the ages they attempted to imitate (in Scott's 1872 design the entrance hall would have been like a monastic undercroft converted into a railway waiting room: what

144

148. The Examination Schools: the vaulted entrance-hall of J. O. Scott's 1875–6 design (*Building News*, 8 Sept. 1876).

149. The Examination Schools: design by Basil Champneys rejected in 1875–6 (*Building News*, 17 Nov. 1876).

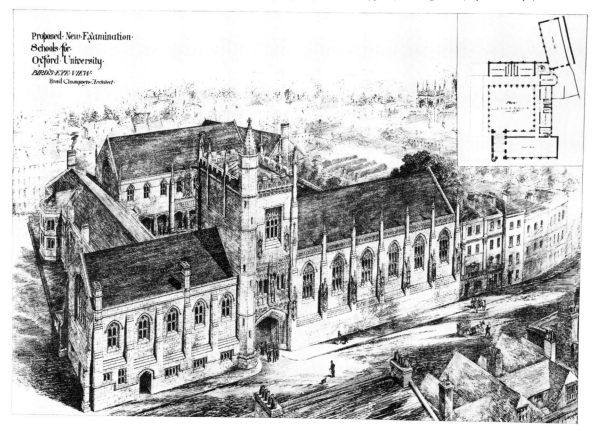

it was like in his 1875 design can be seen from figure 148). The layout is equally undoctrinaire, though less easy to commend. Seen on plan, the entrance hall is awkwardly related to the main building behind it, while the principal staircase, instead of opening out of it, as one would expect, has to be approached by way of a lateral corridor (fig. 150). The main courtyard faces onto a side-street, and

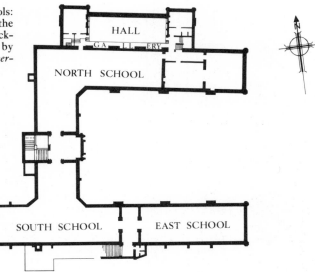

150. The Examination Schools: ground and first-floor plans of the building as erected to T. G. Jackson's designs, 1877–82 (redrawn by Daphne Hart from *Oxford University Gazette*, 7 Jan. 1882).

FIRST FLOOR

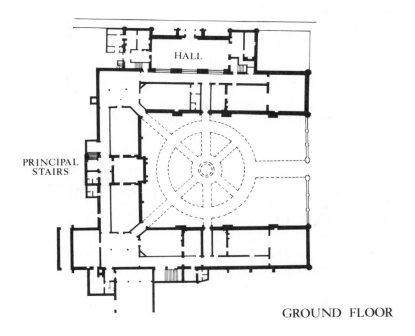

GROUND FLOOR

146

Scale of Metres

Scale of Feet

151. The Examination Schools: the main courtyard from Merton Street.

culminates in a grand tower of superimposed orders that ought to mark an important entrance, but in fact has no practical function at all (fig. 151). Some of these architectural infelicities were, however, due to the difficulties of the site. The entrance hall shields the rooms behind it from the noise of traffic in the street (something to which the Delegates attached particular importance), while the eastern end of the site, between the two wings, could not immediately be built on owing to unexpired leases. The plan that Jackson contrived, though far from elegant, was thought in 1876 to be preferable to any of its quadrangular rivals, and a century's continuous use has done nothing to suggest that the choice was the wrong one.

From the 1870s until the First World War Jackson was almost continuously employed in Oxford. In 1879 he won the commission for the Boys' High School (now the Social Studies Faculty Centre) in competition with the local architects Wilkinson and Codd (fig. 152), but from then onwards he was the University's

147

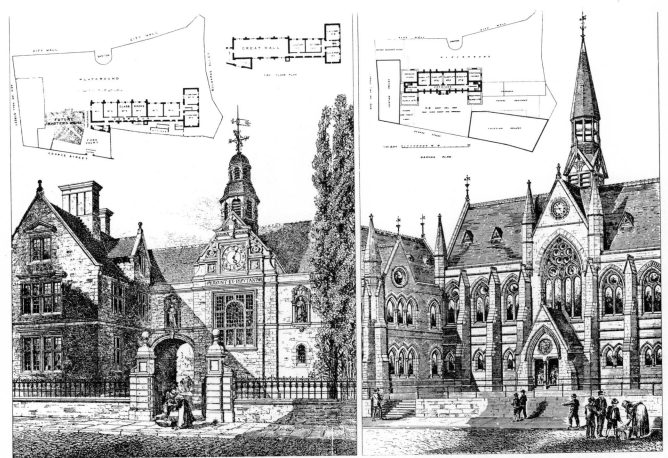

152. The Boys' High School: the designs submitted in 1879 by T. G. Jackson (*left*) and F. Codd (*right*), as illustrated in *Building News*, 19 March 1880. These two designs epitomise the triumph of Jackson's eclectic Jacobethan style over the old doctrinaire Gothic revivalism. Jackson's building is the essence of a picturesque country grammar school – a piece of instant history if ever there was one, infinitely more attractive than Codd's bleak educational institution. Having won the competition Jackson subsequently made his school more symmetrical, whereupon Codd accused him of copying his own design, 'cleverly redressed in Queen Anne's clothes'.

favourite architect (*artifex Oxoniensissimus* as the Public Orator put it in 1911), and could afford to leave competitions to others. His invention never flagged, and his exuberant architecture can be seen all over Oxford. Occasionally it is Gothic (as at Brasenose), more often 'Jacobethan' (as at Corpus, Trinity, the Boys' High School and the King's Mound). Once he tried 'Queen Anne' (at Somerville) and once 'Wrenaissance' (the Electrical Laboratory in the Parks Road). In the Girls' High School he experimented with terra-cotta, in the University Cricket Pavilion with half-timber.

In the course of over thirty years of incessant architectural activity it naturally happened that Jackson made some designs that were not carried out, and others that were considerably modified in execution. Three of the former are illustrated here: a new building for Merton across the street (1878), an alternative design for Trinity (1880), and a steeple to grace the High Street front which he designed for Brasenose (1886). The Merton Scheme (fig. 153) was a standard product of Jackson's office that calls for no special comment. The chief interest of the Trinity

148

153. Merton College: unexecuted design by T. G. Jackson for a new building on the north side of Merton Street, 1878 (Merton College archives).

154. Trinity College: unexecuted design by T. G. Jackson for the front quadrangle, 1880 (Trinity College archives).

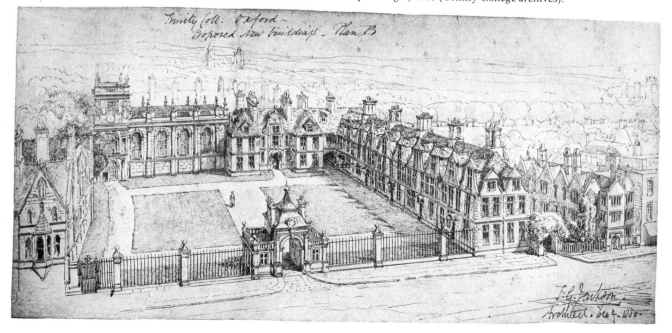

155. Brasenose College: Hawksmoor's design of *circa* 1720, as illustrated in Williams's *Oxonia Depicta* (1732–3).

156. Brasenose College: plan corresponding to figure 155 (Brasenose College archives). The large rectangular building in the middle of the principal quadrangle is the chapel, with the hall immediately behind it.

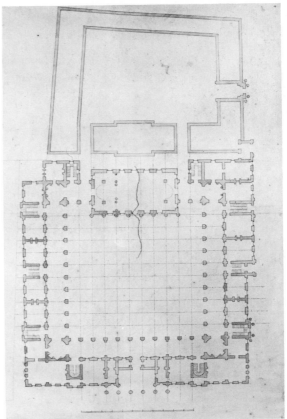

150

one lies in the charming gateway to Broad Street, whose roof echoed one at Westwood Park in Worcestershire (fig. 154). But Brasenose and its steeple demand a section to themselves.

Ever since the eighteenth century Brasenose had been seeking to obtain a frontage, or at least an outlet, onto the High Street. Hawksmoor had envisaged such a development in his plans for Oxford, in which a rebuilt Brasenose was to face a rebuilt All Souls across the new Radcliffe Square. According to an early version of this scheme (*circa* 1712) the south front of the college was to be set well back from the street, thus giving adequate space for a projecting portico and incidentally revealing to view the west end of St. Mary's Church. But in a later version (*circa* 1720) the whole front has been brought forward to the street-line (figs. 155-6). In the 1730s Hawksmoor and Dr. Clarke (who was a graduate of Brasenose) were still wrestling with the problem. As none of the property on the High Street was then at the college's disposal, what they now envisaged was a narrow frontage containing only a gateway and lodges, behind which the Chapel Quadrangle would be enlarged so as to create a classical *atrium* (or colonnaded courtyard) with a new hall on the south side answering to the ante-chapel. From the gateway there would be a vista straight through between the hall and the ante-chapel to the Old Quadrangle (fig. 157). In an alternative plan Hawksmoor shifts the 'Corinthian Atrium' to the south of the chapel, introduces two bell-towers, symmetrically placed on either side of the ante-chapel, and provides 'dry communication' between the two quadrangles by means of a curved cloister or hemicycle. A third scheme dispenses with the *atrium* and divides the new quadrangle between the Principal's garden and the college (fig. 158).

In 1772 the College removed the Principal's Lodgings from the Old Quadrangle into two houses facing onto the High Street, and early in the nineteenth century Sir John Soane was called in, first (1804) to consider the feasibility of adding an upper storey to the Old Quadrangle, and then (1807) of building a new quadrangle to the south. His plan (fig. 159) was far more practical than any of Hawksmoor's, and would have provided the college with a spacious new quadrangle and a substantial addition to its accommodation, including a new Lodging for the Principal and eighteen sets of rooms. Access to those on the east side was to be by means of a vaulted corridor with a vestibule which would doubtless have given Soane an opportunity for some characteristic architectural effects. For the front to the High Street Soane offered two alternative schemes – one in a cumbrous Greek Revival style, the other in a mannered Roman one (fig. 159). Both would clearly have been very expensive, and neither commended itself to the college, which in 1810 considered another, much more moderate, project for a new High Street front in a perfunctory Gothic style (fig. 160). These drawings are signed by Philip Hardwick (1792-1870), then a young man still in his pupilage, and the circumstances in which they were commissioned remain unexplained.

At last in the 1870s the College took effectual steps to acquire the freeholds of the High Street properties and in 1880 Jackson was engaged to design a new quadrangle that could be built in stages. As the loss of rents from the houses and

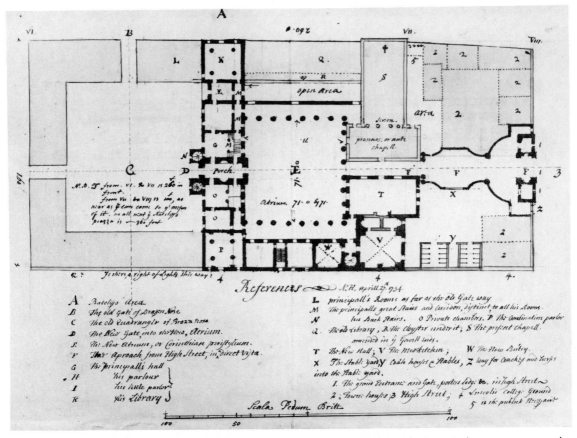

157. Brasenose College: a plan made by Hawksmoor in 1734, retaining the old chapel, squeezing a new gateway in between the houses on the High Street (at right), and introducing a Corinthian *atrium* or colonnaded court in the middle of the college (Brasenose College archives).

158. Brasenose College: another plan made by Hawksmoor in 1734, retaining the old chapel, but dispensing with the 'atrium' and dividing the new central quadrangle between the Principal's garden (above) and the college (below) (Brasenose College archives).

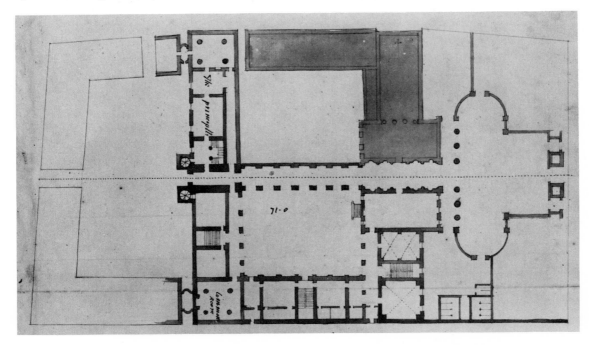

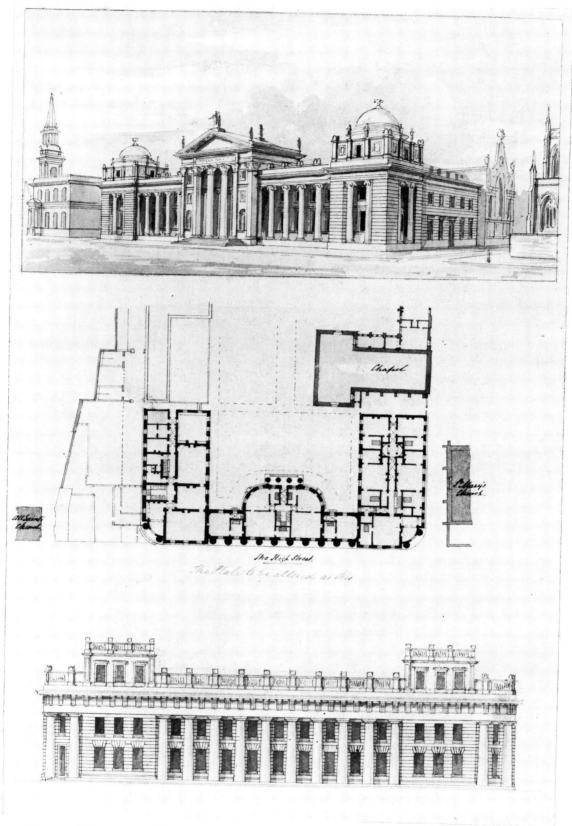

159. Brasenose College: designs for a new High Street frontage made by John Soane in 1807. *Above*, elevation in the Roman style. *Centre and below*, plan and elevation in the Greek Doric style (Bodleian Library, G. A. Oxon. a.49, p.28).

160. Brasenose College: proposed elevation to High Street in the Gothic style submitted by Philip Hardwick in 1810 (Brasenose College archives).

shops now to be demolished was a matter of some concern to the college Jackson's first design was for a frontage with shops on the ground floor and college rooms above. In the end this was abandoned, and instead he was encouraged to make the entrance tower into a prominent feature of the High Street. 'This', Jackson recalled, 'presented several still more difficult problems. The steeples of St. Mary's and All Saints' are not very far apart, and the street thereabouts is not curved, but straight; it is consequently very difficult to put a large tower between them so that it shall not clash with either or both of them from some point of view. After many trials, not only on paper, but with flags and scaffold poles, I managed this by placing the tower not in the façade but behind it, projecting a little into the quadrangle; and this forced me, in order to show it to the front, to run it up to a height rivalling the two other steeples ... The proper form for the tower was another difficulty; for a square tower of the usual collegiate type would not do between the two church steeples; and, again, a steeple would be too ecclesiastical an ornament for a college.' Eventually he decided in favour of an openwork 'crown' of the sort familiar from King's College at Aberdeen and St. Nicholas' Church in Newcastle, 'which seemed to give the pointed form necessary to harmony with its neighbours, while avoiding by its openness the heaviness of a simple tower' (fig. 161). However, partly for reasons of cost, the steeple was abandoned and in its stead Jackson designed a gateway of the normal Oxford type, but with royal arms and supporters over the outer arch in the Cambridge manner (fig. 162). When the quadrangle was finally completed in 1911, Jackson congratulated himself, not unjustifiably, on having built something that was 'worthy of the most important site in the most beautiful street in Europe'.

Although for a quarter of a century Jackson was Oxford's most favoured architect, he by no means monopolised the commissions offered by either university or city. St. John's preferred to employ G.G. Scott, junior, Magdalen and University College Bodley and Garner, New College and Oriel Basil Champneys. In 1891 Jackson did not compete for the new Town Hall, but it was a tribute to his own success in establishing the fashion for neo-mannerist architecture in Oxford that the winning design, by H.T. Hare, should have been as exuberantly Jacobean as anything of Jackson's own. In the university Jackson's principal rival, Basil Champneys (1842–1935), was not only an accomplished designer in a distinctive late Gothic manner (as at New College, 1885 onwards, Mansfield, 1887–9, and Merton, 1904–10), but also the purveyor of his own variety of Jacobean (Indian Institute, 1883–96, Somerville Library, 1902–3, Oriel, Rhodes Building, 1908–11, and Merton, Warden's Lodgings, 1908). And in North Oxford house after red-brick house shows in quaint mask or minuscule broken pediment how H.W. Moore (1850–1915) was endeavouring to give a touch of mannerist charm to elevations which twenty years earlier would have been as gauntly Gothic as his former partner Wilkinson could make them.

161. Brasenose College: Jackson's original scheme for the High Street front, with an entrance tower set back from the street and surmounted by an openwork 'crown' (Brasenose College archives).

162. Brasenose College: the High Street front built to T. G. Jackson's designs in 1881–9 and 1909–11.

155

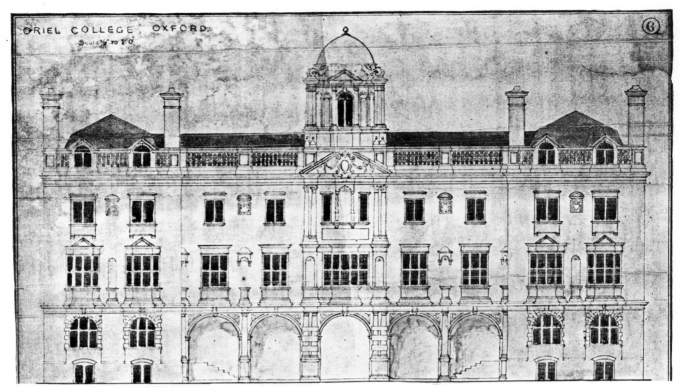

163. Oriel College: the Rhodes Building as first proposed by Basil Champneys, with an open arcade to the High Street, domed central feature and balustraded parapet. The left-hand block and much of the centre was to be given up to a new Provost's Lodging, and the five windows on the first floor above the arcade were to light a gallery belonging to the Lodging. The college eventually decided to retain the existing Provost's Lodging and demanded detailing 'more in accordance with the style which has become traditional in Oxford' (Oriel College archives).

164. Oriel College: the Rhodes Building as built in 1909-11.

156

The Rhodes Building at Oriel (figs. 163-4) was the last monument of the Jacobean Revival in Oxford. What succeeded it was the 'Wrenaissance' style introduced by Sir Reginald Blomfield at Lady Margaret Hall in 1896, and promptly adopted by Jackson himself in the Electrical Laboratory of 1908-10. The transition from neo-mannerist to neo-baroque (and ultimately to neo-Georgian) occasioned no such controversy as those of the previous century, and has (so far as I am aware) left no similar legacy of defeated designs to illustrate this book. In place of the eager patronage of the eighteenth century and the impassioned if often perverse aesthetic commitment of the nineteenth, all that early twentieth-century Oxford could offer was a complacent conformity to what it fondly imagined to be its own architectural tradition.

X

Oxford and the Modern Movement

IN VICTORIAN OXFORD – as the last two chapters have shown – architecture was taken seriously. Competitions were held for the major commissions, and nearly all the leading Victorian architects were at one time or another invited to submit designs; designs whose merits and demerits were widely canvassed. In 1854, as the university official G. V. Cox recalled in his reminiscences, 'the interest excited [by the designs for the Museum] was immense, and the question "Gothic or Grecian?" was everywhere discussed'. In 1869–76 it took three delegacies and half-a-dozen architects seven years to produce a design for the Examination Schools that was acceptable to Convocation. The results of these contests were generally creditable to the university. The Museum was a landmark of the Gothic Revival, the Schools of the Jacobean one that followed it, while the Ashmolean was among the finest neo-classical buildings in Britain. In the colleges Bodley and Garner, Butterfield, Jackson, Champneys and G.G. Scott all left distinguished examples of their respective interpretations of residential Gothic. The Victorian university could on the whole congratulate itself on its architectural patronage: certainly the architectural historian can admire the notable additions it made to the anthology of Gothic buildings of every shape and form that is Oxford's architectural speciality.

This concern for architecture was by no means a natural product of an academic environment dedicated, as it was, to a culture essentially literary and non-visual. Rather it must be seen as a legacy of the religious controversies of the 1840s and 1850s, in which ritualism and Gothic architecture had been so important an element. Thanks to the ecclesiologists a knowledge of the succeeding styles of Gothic architecture could be taken for granted in a predominantly clerical society like that of Oxford, in much the same way as a knowledge of the classical orders could be taken for granted among educated men in the previous century. Once it was established (by propagandists like Pugin and Ruskin) that architecture was an expression of morality, then a general – sometimes, indeed, an impassioned – interest in architectural issues was guaranteed. The 'Oxford Society for promoting the study of Gothic Architecture', founded in 1839, was a pressure-group which counted among its early members nine bishops, many heads of houses, several professors and numerous fellows of colleges. So in Victorian Oxford, when architectural drawings were exhibited before a vote was taken, they were scrutin-ised by those who had some standards by which to judge them. Those standards were, no doubt, ones that sometimes seem to us perverse, but if morality often dominated aesthetics, aesthetic preferences often masqueraded as moral impera-tives, and what mattered was that architectural issues were seen to be of general concern. By the end of the century, however, the clerical monopoly of fellowships had been broken, the religious controversies of the past had largely been forgotten, the Oxford Society had abandoned its high purpose for ordinary antiquarian pursuits, and nothing new had emerged that could be counted on to stimulate an interest in contemporary architecture. In an academic world that was becoming increasingly professional, architecture could hope to command the attention of senior members of the university only by becoming itself a subject of study. But of this there was little prospect in a university dedicated to training the intellect rather than the eye and as suspicious as its medieval predecessor of anything 'mechanical' or 'applied'. As for junior members, they followed their tutors' example: not once in its whole history has the Oxford Union Society held a debate on an architectural issue.

In 1910, in a prescient pamphlet entitled *Can we not save Architecture in Oxford?*, E.W.B. Nicholson, then Bodley's Librarian, expressed concern about the lack of architecturally informed opinion in the university. What particularly disturbed him was the number of ill-judged schemes to solve the problem of over-crowding in the Bodleian Library. (They included filling up the north and south sides of the Schools Quadrangle level with the projecting staircases, glazing over the quadrangle, building a wing right across it, or extending it either south towards the Radcliffe Library or north towards the Clarendon Building.) What he advocated was the establishment of a professorship of architecture, or of an 'Architectural Board', or perhaps of 'a consulting architect to the University elected by Congregation'. No notice was, of course, taken of these suggestions, but over thirty years later, at the close of the Second World War, at a time when money for new chairs was forthcoming from government, the Board of the Faculty of Modern History expressed a desire for a Professor of the History of Architecture and the matter was seriously considered by the Hebdomadal Council. Unfortu-nately nothing came of it, and not every historian of architecture is necessarily interested in contemporary issues. But a Summerson, or a Pevsner, or even a Geoffrey Webb (to name three likely candidates for the chair) might well have become something of an architectural mentor to his immediate colleagues and perhaps to the university at large.

As it was, most Oxford dons of the early twentieth century were as determinedly indifferent to contemporary developments in architecture as their predecessors had been to classical architecture in the early seventeenth century. Their minds were attuned to beauties other than architectural: to beauties literary, logical, musical, scientific, but not structural or three-dimensional. Gothic cathedrals, of course, they visited during the vacation, and classical architecture they admired in foreign countries. But at home architecture was something one did not normally meddle with, and if a new building became necessary, then, being a professional one's self, one employed another professional.*

To appreciate this architectural indifference or non-commitment one needs only to spend an afternoon walking round the Oxford suburbs where the married dons of the 1920s and 1930s lived. Headington and Boar's Hill are not the places to find avant-garde architecture. The one exception is the house on Hinksey Hill built by Ellis Waterhouse in 1939 to the designs of Samuel and Harding: unassertive, but indubitably 'modern', it is the sole reflection in Oxford of the aesthetic revolution that had overtaken European architecture since the First World War. Nor do the more traditional houses of the same period suggest any conscious repudiation of the 'Modern Movement' in favour of a discriminating adherence to older architectural values. On the contrary, they are conventional products of inter-war architecture, such as one might find in any well-to-do London suburb. Only in Belbroughton Road will the connoisseur of neo-Georgian find a small group of houses worth his attention, but they were not commissioned by senior members of the university. They were a private speculative development (*circa* 1925) by a professional architect called Christopher Wright.

It has been necessary to emphasise the degree to which early twentieth-century Oxford was out of touch with contemporary architectural thought to introduce the reader to the two unexecuted schemes, for Balliol and All Souls Colleges, that are here illustrated. Both were as revolutionary as anything in Oxford's architectural history and would, if executed, have been among the key buildings of the 'Modern Movement' in England. In the architecturally conservative university of the 1930s there was little chance that either of them would be carried out, but they were the first intimation that even in Oxford men had at least heard of the new architecture towards which Le Corbusier was so plausibly beckoning them.

The Balliol scheme dates from 1936 and it was due to one man. His name was Kenneth Bell and he was a tutor (in Modern History) whose life was devoted to his college and his pupils. The Balliol Society, the Balliol College Education Trust, the Holywell Manor annexe, were all due to his foresight and initiative. No sooner was the Manor established as an offshoot of the college than Bell's restless energy fixed on the idea of increasing the accommodation in the college itself. He was not, it seems, especially interested in architecture, but anything that would redound to the greater glory of Balliol was close to his heart, and a new hall in a new style was an idea to conjure with. It so happened that a Balliol man called Godfrey Samuel had been a member of the Tecton Group formed in 1932 by the Russian architect Lubetkin. Samuel had recently established practice on his own with Valentine Harding, another member of the Tecton office, and so it was

* President Blakiston of Trinity is, however, known to have played a large part in designing that College's classical library in 1925-7, and in 1936 the versatile Frederick Soddy, Professor of Chemistry, volunteered a scheme for extending Exeter College over the site of Parker's bookshop. It was cleverly planned, but the kidney-shaped eight-storey tower-block that he envisaged, surmounted by an open turret, would have been a precursor in Broad Street of the 'Botley Skylon'.

160

Samuel and Harding to whom Bell went for designs. The result was a scheme to build a new hall on the site of the Master's Lodgings, and to replace the existing hall (a detached Gothic building by Waterhouse) by a new residential block. In this way the amount of accommodation in the college would be substantially increased. Only the designs for the hall were worked out in any detail (figs. 165–6). With their simple clear-cut forms they express forcibly their authors' distaste for a century's accumulated architectural clutter. They also exemplify very clearly the principle of formal discipline that Lubetkin had inculcated in his pupils. Here are no arbitrary curves or accidental asymmetries. Everything is as taut and precise in its way as if it were controlled by a classical order: indeed in the interior, the upright members between the windows have something of the character of an order. Externally, the juxtaposition of glass walls and Gothic masonry would have been brutally abrupt (figs. 167–8). Even so it might have been worth while sacrificing the gloomy Master's Lodgings to have had this crisp and elegant building in its place. But having already committed itself to Holywell Manor, the college was in no mood for a further architectural venture, and the whole scheme was fairly summarily dismissed by Bell's colleagues.

All Souls' aspirations were much less grandiose, but by no means simple. What the college required was an enlargement of the Common Room, a new house or flat for the Manciple (or resident steward), and six or more sets of rooms for fellows. The site available (that of the existing Manciple's house) was constricted and awkwardly hemmed in between the kitchen on the west, the Warden's garden on the south, and Queen's College on the east. Service access from the High Street to the kitchen had to be maintained, the amenities of the Warden's garden preserved, and the view from Queen's respected. In 1930 A.S.G. Butler, then the college's established architect, was asked to address himself to the problem. His solution was to build a new block in neo-Georgian style which would mirror an enlarged Warden's Lodging and to link the two buildings by a Doric loggia (figs. 169–170). Though Butler's classical detailing was pleasant enough, the resultant duality would have been awkward and the total effect a little pretentious. Nothing was done, and in 1937 the college decided to start afresh and to hold a limited competition. A 'modernist' party now made itself felt, consisting of Richard Pares, Geoffrey Hudson and Stuart Hampshire (later Warden of Wadham). On their insistence two modern architects were invited to submit designs: Maxwell Fry (recently in partnership with Walter Gropius of Bauhaus fame) and Messrs. Scott, Shepherd and Breakwell, the architects of the Shakespeare Memorial Theatre at Stratford. The third competitor was W.G. Newton, son of Ernest Newton, and a competent but unremarkable traditionalist who two years later was to design the Nuffield Building at Worcester College. In due course the sub-committee had before it a steel-framed scheme by Fry, four (in part five) storeys high, and flexibly planned to make the most of the awkward site (figs. 171–2); a much less assertive proposal by Scott, Shepherd and Breakwell for low ranges of an unassuming modern character with white walls and roofs either flat or pitched; and a design by Newton for some modest neo-Georgian buildings weakly detailed in a manner

165, 166. (*facing page*) Balliol College: designs for a new hall by Samuel and Harding, 1936 (Balliol College archives).

167. Balliol College: the Broad Street front of the new hall proposed by Samuel and Harding in 1936 (Balliol College archives).

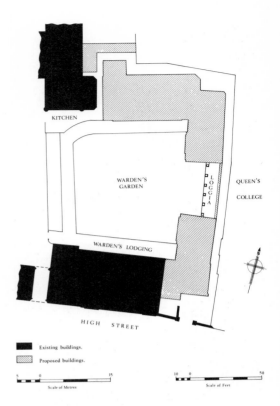

168. Balliol College: a general view of Samuel and Harding's scheme, showing in the foreground the proposed new hall and in the background the Victorian hall replaced by a new residential block (Balliol College archives).

169. All Souls College: plan showing A. S. G. Butler's design for a neo-Georgian block behind the Warden's Lodgings, 1930 (based on a plan in All Souls College archives).

170. All Souls College: south elevation of A. S. G. Butler's design of 1930. The hall and kitchen are on the left, and on the right the proposed loggia is seen in section (All Souls College archives).

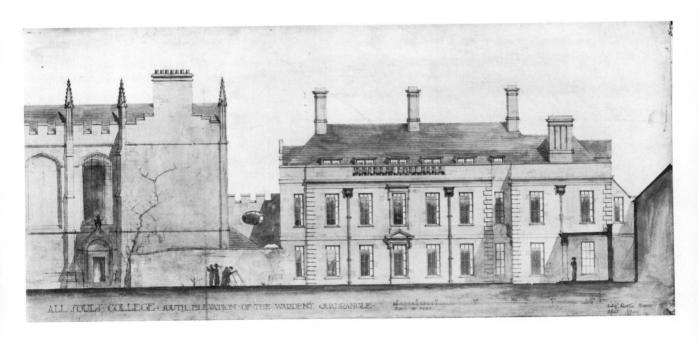

164

171. All Souls College: a perspective of Maxwell Fry's design of 1937, seen from the south-west (All Souls College archives).

172. All Souls College: aerial perspective of Maxwell Fry's design of 1937, with the Warden's Lodgings at bottom left (All Souls College archives).

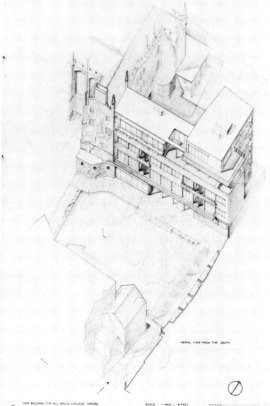

165

not entirely free from the contaminating influence of Worthington.* In November 1938 the Governing Body preferred Scott, Shepherd and Breakwell's design as a compromise between Maxwell Fry's glass-house and Newton's dull traditionalism. But the voting was not decisive, and the college decided to seek a further design from Morley Horder before making up its mind. In the event the war supervened and the whole scheme was shelved, to be revived in 1946–7 and 1951–2, in which years designs by C.H. James and Edward Maufe were successively commissioned, approved and then refused a licence at a time when building materials were still in short supply and their use severely restricted. By now the college had lost all enthusiasm for the 'Modern Movement', and wanted a building 'which would harmonize with the Warden's Lodgings and other adjacent buildings, perhaps of an "Annish" style'. What they got from James was late Georgian rather than 'Annish' in style, very dull in elevation, and awkwardly irregular in plan. Maufe's design (fig. 173) was a standard product of his office intended (in his own words) 'to have the character of a Country House'. But for neither scheme was a licence forthcoming, and in the end the college had to content itself with a modest remodelling of the existing buildings on the site. To the architectural historian the interest of the whole episode lies chiefly in Maxwell Fry's uncompromising design for a building in the International Style of the 1920s and 1930s, with characteristic flat roofs, wide ribbon windows and casually asymmetrical elevations. In his report he claimed that the stylistic clash involved was no more violent than the change from medieval to Georgian in the High Street front of the college. What he failed to point out was that both the fifteenth- and the eighteenth-century portions of the college consist of load-bearing stone walls with a high proportion of solid to void, whereas his thin strips of cladding (even if of stone in some form), suspended between continuous ribbons of glass, would have belonged to a different technological and aesthetic world altogether. Whatever its merits, Fry's building would have been an alien architectural presence within the walls of All Souls, and the failure to build it need hardly be regretted.†

The most notable architectural casualty of the 1930s was, however, a building that was neither a characteristic product of the 'Modern Movement', nor a conventional design in the manner of A.S.G. Butler or W.G. Newton. This was Austen Harrison's design for Nuffield College.

In October 1937 Lord Nuffield, the creator of one of the most flourishing industrial enterprises of his time, gave £900,000 to the University in order to build and endow a new college that was to be devoted primarily to research in the field of social studies. In the formal letter to the Vice-Chancellor in which he outlined this gift, Lord Nuffield recalled that it had 'long been my desire to improve the aspect of the approach to Oxford from the west', and that it was 'with

* For whom see below, p. 177.

† In March 1937 Christ's College, Cambridge, rejected a very similar design by Gropius and Fry for a new block in Hobson Street. It is illustrated by Booth & Taylor, *Cambridge New Architecture* (1970), p. 14.

TO THE SOUTH AND THE WARDEN'S GARDEN

173. All Souls College: a neo-Georgian design by Edward Maufe for the same site, submitted in 1951 (R.I.B.A. Drawings Collection). The carving in the pediment was to represent the college totem, a male duck or mallard. Flanking the building are swans, birds heraldically associated with the college's founder, Archbishop Chichele.

that object' that he had 'recently purchased the large canal-wharf which lies to the north of the New Road in the hope that part [of it] . . . might become the site of some University building of an appropriate kind, to fill the gap between Worcester College and Pembroke College'. This piece of land he now offered as the site for the new college. It was, therefore, with architectural improvement as well as academic development in mind that Lord Nuffield became the founder of an Oxford college.

The college, as an independent corporate body consisting of a Warden and Fellows, did not come into existence until after the War. It was the University, as the immediate recipient of Lord Nuffield's gift, that had the responsibility for planning and erecting the buildings. A committee was set up for the purpose, and in December 1937 a sub-committee was appointed to select an architect. The members of this sub-committee were Sir William Beveridge (Master of University College), the Principal of St. Edmund Hall (A.B. Emden) and the Principal of Lady Margaret Hall (Miss Linda Grier). Of the three Emden was probably the best informed architecturally, and appears to have taken the leading role. At first the sub-committee thought of holding a limited competition, suggesting the names of five architects: Louis de Soissons, Curtis Green, Vincent Harris, Edward Maufe and Hubert Worthington, plus Connell, Ward and Lucas on the ground

167

that 'the modernists ought to be given a chance'. But in the end, after consideration of a wider field (which included 'three architects of outstanding reputation, Holden, Lutyens and Scott'), the choice was narrowed down to Louis de Soissons, J.M. Easton, Vincent Harris, Austen Harrison, Charles Holden, C.H. James, Edward Maufe, V.O. Rees, R. Uren and Hubert Worthington. Holden and Maufe, on being approached, both declined to be considered, the latter stating that he had too much work in hand to take on anything more. The others submitted photographs of their work, and on this basis (plus some personal inspection of buildings) the sub-committee expressed a strong interest in Harrison, until recently Government Architect in Palestine, whose name had been suggested by Sir Arthur Salter, the Gladstone Professor of Government, and whose referees included Eric Gill, C.R. Ashbee and Sir Ronald Storrs.* Harrison, though a graduate of the School of Architecture at University College, London, and a Fellow of the R.I.B.A., had never practised in Britain, and all his executed works were either in Greece or in Palestine. His public buildings in the latter country, which included the Government House and the Archaeological Museum in Jerusalem and the Governor's House in Amman, were formally designed in a bold round-arched style that was half Romanesque and half oriental in character. Striking though they were, it is difficult to see what it was in these buildings that persuaded the committee that Harrison was the best man to design a new college in Oxford. However an interview confirmed their choice, and on 17 June 1938 Harrison was given the commission. He immediately entered into partnership with two younger men who were to act as his assistants, named T.S. Barnes and R.P.S. Hubbard.

The building that Harrison was asked to envisage was more than just a college, with its hall, chapel, warden's lodging and sets for fellows, students and visiting scholars: there was also to be a large institute for research in the social sciences, with a library, lecture theatre, conference rooms, seminar rooms, and so forth. From Harrison's preliminary studies it soon became apparent that all this could not satisfactorily be provided on the original site, so Lord Nuffield made available an extra piece of land on the west side of Worcester Street. On this Harrison

* Austen St. Barbe Harrison was born in Kent in 1891. As a young man he went to Canada, studied architecture at McGill University, Montreal, and worked in the vacations in the office of Robert Findlay, a leading Montreal architect of Scottish birth. Leaving McGill without graduating, he transferred in 1913 to the School of Architecture at University College, London, where he was placed in the first class in the Intermediate Examination (1914). After the First World War he was appointed Assistant Architect and Town Planner in the Department of Reconstruction for Eastern Macedonia, in which capacity he planned Nigrita and other towns and villages to house Greek refugees from Asia Minor. In 1923 he became Chief Architect to the Department of Public Works in Palestine, then under the British Mandate, and designed a number of public buildings in Jerusalem, Jaffa, Amman, etc. Later he made a report (published in 1945) on the planning of Valletta, Malta, and designed the University of Ghana in West Africa. He lived in Cyprus (where his conversation and style of life reminded Lawrence Durrell of 'the hero of *South Wind* or an early character from Huxley') and latterly in Athens, where he died in 1976. Nuffield College appears to have been his only architectural work in the British Isles.

proposed to build the institute and its satellite buildings, leaving the whole of the main site free for the residential part of the college. The plan that now formed itself in the architect's mind was of a strictly formal character, based on the intersection of two axes, one dominated by the hall and its staircase tower, the other by the warden's lodging to the north and the chapel to the south (figs. 174–6). The main entrance was to be at the west end of the longer axis, where, after

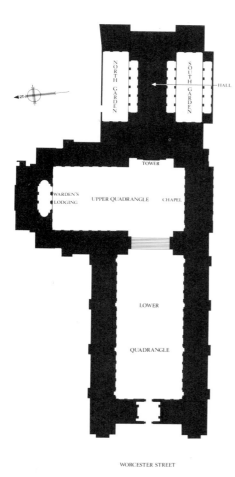

174. Nuffield College: general plan of Harrison's first design of 1938, showing how the college proper was to be separated from the institute for social studies by Worcester Street. The semi-circular plan of the garage-block suggests that Harrison may have had in mind the well-known bus-garage in Moscow designed by the Russian architect Melnikov in 1926, which was similarly planned (redrawn by Daphne Hart from plans in Nuffield College archives).

169

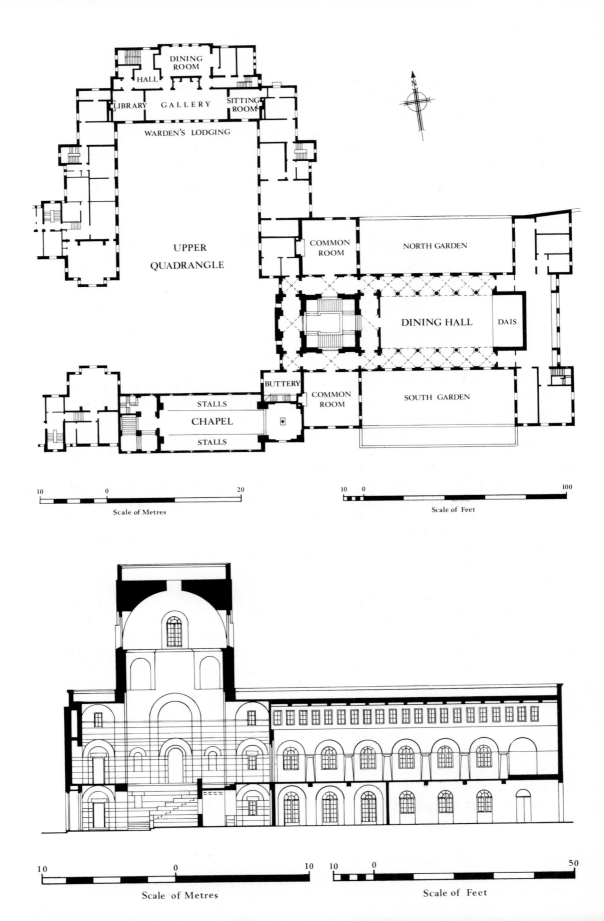

DINING
ROOM

HALL

LIBRARY   G A L L E R Y   SITTING
ROOM

WARDEN'S LODGING

UPPER

QUADRANGLE

COMMON
ROOM

NORTH GARDEN

DINING HALL   DAIS

BUTTERY

STALLS

CHAPEL   COMMON
ROOM   SOUTH GARDEN

STALLS

10   0   20
Scale of Metres

10   0   100
Scale of Feet

10   0   10   10   0   50

Scale of Metres   Scale of Feet

the visitor had passed through the porter's lodge, his eye would at once be focussed on the tower, seen in perspective beyond the flight of steps which separated the two quadrangles (fig. 177). Having traversed the length of the lower quadrangle and mounted the steps, the visitor would perceive on his left the subsidiary façade of the Warden's Lodging, with its open loggia on the ground floor, and on his right the answering façade of the chapel. The relationship between the principal buildings was elegantly worked out, and in a university of self-contained spaces the intersecting axes on two levels represented an innovation in planning that was highly effective.

If the general layout was for Oxford a novel one, the stylistic treatment was even more so. Anyone looking at the plan would relate it to the 'Beaux-Arts' tradition and expect architecture of a classical character. But although invariably symmetrical, the elevations were to be totally devoid of any overtly classical detailing, and their stark external walls, flat roofs and cubical forms (to be carried out in white Portland stone) would have given the whole building a strongly Mediterranean character. In fact the detailing was largely derived from medieval buildings in the Mediterranean area with which Harrison was familiar. The great semi-circular doorway at the main entrance, with its facetted voussoirs (fig. 179) came from the Muslim world via Norman Sicily. Externally the tower was to rise to a polygonal upper storey, inside which there was to be a dome supported on squinches or pendentives in a manner common to Islam, Byzantium and parts of Southern France. The hall was to be aisled like a basilica, with plain round arches on either side supported on stumpy 'primitive' columns more Greek Doric than Romanesque in character. The common rooms were never fully worked out, but Harrison's sketches indicate decoration of a frankly oriental type, with hooded fireplaces such as those in the Topkapi Palace in Istanbul. As for the chapel, it was to have the character of a barrel-vaulted crypt, with light filtering in from unseen windows in a manner that might have been either numinous or claustro-phobic, but was certainly better suited to bright Mediterranean sunlight than the dull latitude of Oxford.

In many ways it was an impressive design, effectively exploiting an awkwardly elongated site, and creating a building which would have taken its place among the major architectural monuments of Oxford. The library complex across the road would have exceeded in its size and facilities every other faculty or dependent library then existing (and most of those built since). The Warden's Lodging would have been one of the most handsome and commodious of its kind, and the grand staircase and the hieratic hall to which it led would have rivalled those of Christ Church itself (Fig. 176). But there was little that was English, still less that was recognisably Oxonian, about the design, and sooner or later someone was bound to express surprise and perhaps disquiet at the great white building that Harrison proposed to set down in the western outskirts of the city. How far the committee fully understood the architect's intentions we do not know. But early in 1939 they recommended the adoption of his plans, and in the course of the summer these were shown to Lord Nuffield in the form of a large model.

171

175. (*facing page, above*) Nuffield College: first-floor plan of the upper quadrangle in Harrison's first design of 1938 (redrawn by Daphne Hart from a plan in Nuffield College archives).

176. (*facing page, below*) Nuffield College: section of the aisled hall and staircase tower in Harrison's first design of 1938 (redrawn by Daphne Hart from the original in Nuffield College archives).

177. Nuffield College: view from the west end of the lower quadrangle as proposed in Harrison's first design of 1938 (drawn by Paul Draper).

178. Nuffield College: the same view in 1982.

179. Nuffield College: the entrance-front as proposed in Harrison's first design of 1938 (from a model in porcelain by Hugh Colvin). Although Siculo-Norman in detailing, the great semi-circular doorway suggests the influence of the American architect H. H. Richardson, of whose work such doorways are a characteristic feature.

Although Lord Nuffield had given his assent to Harrison's appointment there had been no subsequent consultation with him about the architectural character of the college that was to bear his name. It was generally known that he wanted something in the Oxford collegiate tradition, but the committee did not think fit to fetter the architect by any stipulation as to period or style. The 'Oxford tradition' was, after all, capable of many interpretations. They ought, however, to have realised that Harrison's interpretation was very far removed from what most people regarded as characteristic of Oxford's architecture. So when Lord Nuffield contemplated the model that the architect set down before him – a model made unprepossessingly of clay, without any of those little artifices by which modern architects beguile their clients – he was dismayed to see flat roofs instead of pitched ones, and to find a bald, 'factory-like' elevation to the street, instead of the mellow and picturesque group of buildings that he had hoped to see rising on the north side of the New Road. Even the tower was devoid of all the conventional ornamentation of battlements and pinnacles that he associated with its kind. Was this the building by which he was to be remembered, the tribute to Oxford's past glories by which he was to atone in the west of the city for the environmental damage that his factories had done in the east? The more he contemplated the model the more he disliked it and the more he feared that it would attract the same sort of unfavourable criticism as the New Bodleian (whose uncouth mass, recently revealed, had just been the subject of some scathing verses by Neville Coghill in the *Oxford Magazine*). An interview with the Vice-Chancellor (A.D. Lindsay, Master of Balliol) did nothing to modify his wrath and on the following day he wrote formally to disown the design:

Morris Motors Ltd.
Cowley, Oxford
15 August 1939

My dear Vice-Chancellor,
    In confirmation of what passed at our interview yesterday, I write to say that,

173

after careful consideration, I feel obliged to adhere to my adverse judgement of the plans submitted for Nuffield College.

I consider the design to be un-English and out of keeping with the best tradition of Oxford architecture; as well as contrary to my expressed wishes that it should be in conformity with that tradition. Indeed, I go so far as to say that, if a building of this type were to be erected, I would not allow my name to be associated therewith.

> Yours sincerely,
> NUFFIELD

From a Founder's letter, couched in such terms, there could be no appeal. It was in vain that Harrison pointed out that the 'Oxford tradition' in architecture was a vague and indeterminate concept, that whatever characteristics colleges had in common (such as 'Halls and Common Rooms adapted to a gregarious life at once simple, spacious and ritualistic') it was not expressed in any uniformity of architectural style, but rather in a quadrangular type of plan which he had duly adopted. For the rest the 'Oxford tradition' was no more than a picturesque 'accidentalism' that was due to the modifications and accretions of centuries and to the effects of dirt and decay – both of which it would be absurd to try to achieve in a new building. As it was, he insisted that his design was far from being a typical example of twentieth-century architecture. It was only by a compromise that one could hope 'to please at once a 20th century donor with an industrial background who sighs for romance, a committee of economists who are after results [and] the governing committee of a University steeped in its tradition'. But these protestations were of no avail. The Founder had spoken, and the committee, having failed to consult him in time, could now only bow to his wishes.

At this point the committee might have been tempted to dismiss Harrison and find another architect who was better qualified to design the kind of building that Lord Nuffield wanted: in 1939 there were still a few architects in practice who understood the vocabulary of English traditional architecture and were capable of handling it with assurance. Sir Giles Scott was one of them, and despite the débâcle of the New Bodleian, Lord Nuffield wrote on 22 April to recommend his employment. But Harrison expressed his willingness to try to meet Lord Nuffield's wishes with 'something on the lines of Cotswold domestic architecture' and the committee decided to give him another chance. The result was the design illustrated in figure 180. Beneath the pitched roofs with their gable-ends and dormer windows, the general layout was fundamentally the same. But the formality of the planning had been modified. The hall was now at ground level, making the grand staircase unnecessary, and its character was entirely changed: it was now a single space without aisles and it was roofed in traditional English manner with hammer-beam trusses of oak timber. The tower, deprived of the staircase which had been its original *raison d'être*, had been moved off the principal axis to a position immediately east of the chapel, where it housed the common room on the ground floor before soaring up on open arches to support an octagonal lantern and a short spire. The main entrance was now on the south side beneath the

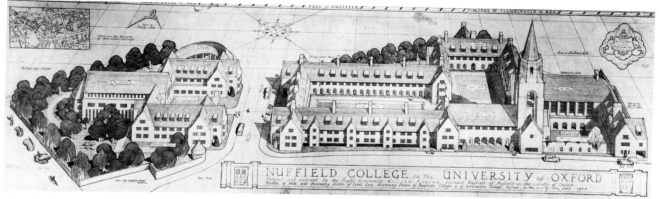

180. Nuffield College: Harrison's second design of 1939 (University Surveyor's Office).

chapel, and took the form of an arcaded vestibule supported by columns of Byzantine character. This was in deference to Lord Nuffield's expressed wish that it should be possible for the passer-by to get a glimpse of the quadrangle from the street. Although the perfunctory detailing of the gables and dormer windows betrayed Harrison's ignorance of English vernacular building, the general effect was certainly picturesque, and enough survived from the original design to make it much more than just a half-hearted essay in 'Cotswold domestic architecture'. In the spring of 1940 Lord Nuffield signified his approval, subject only to the substitution for the spired steeple of a more conventional tower. 'I fancy (wrote the Vice-Chancellor after a meeting with Nuffield) that, apart from the squaring, he would like pinnacles, as on the top of Magdalen Tower'.

By now, however, the country was at war, and it was clear that by the time building again became possible, inflation would seriously have diminished the value of the capital endowment provided by Lord Nuffield. A substantial reduction in accommodation had already been achieved in the revised scheme, but by the end of the war it was evident that further and more drastic economies would be necessary. A model made early in 1949 (when the foundation stone was finally laid) showed the tower reduced in height, deprived of its spire in accordance with the Founder's wishes, and terminated by an octagonal lantern (fig. 181). The main entrance has been simplified, and the arcaded treatment that had from the first been a characteristic feature of the internal elevations has been abandoned, much to their detriment. As the work progressed in stages, first the chapel was dispensed with, together with the triple entrance beneath it, and then the library complex across the road was postponed to an indefinite future. At last, in 1956, the tower was completed as an up-ended bookstack, a utilitarian function which accorded ill with its originally ornamental purpose, necessitating a repetitive uniformity of fenestration to which the architects failed to find a satisfactory solution. Its rectangular bulk was, however, relieved by a *flèche*, a feature for which several alternative designs were made, varying in style from Rhenish Romanesque to American colonial (fig. 182). The one eventually adopted makes its contribution to the Oxford skyline without any overt reference to historical precedent, and is

175

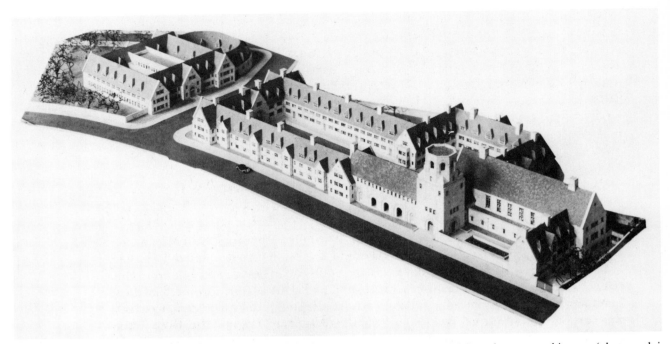

181. Nuffield College: model made in 1949, showing the reduced design upon the basis of which work was started in 1949 (photograph in Nuffield College Library).

182. Nuffield College: alternative designs for the termination of the tower made in 1954 (Nuffield College archives).

similar in character to the one proposed in 1940 (fig. 183). But, one by one, all the other features that had given Harrison's original design its interest and distinction had been dropped, and only two vestiges of it can still be discerned today. One is the two cardinal axes, no longer focussed on major architectural incidents, but still arousing an expectation of formality to which the 'Cotswold' architecture sadly fails to respond. The other is the form of the principal doorways, whose carefully-cut masonry exhibits that peculiar combination of semi-circular intrados and ogival extrados which was a mark, not of Tudor England, but of medieval Italy and some other parts of the Mediterranean world whose architecture Harrison had once dreamed of transplanting to twentieth-century Oxford.

While Balliol and All Souls were shutting their doors to the 'Modern Movement' and Harrison was losing his battle with Lord Nuffield, two architects were quietly establishing Oxford practices for themselves. Their names were Hubert Worthington and Edward Maufe. Worthington's father had designed Manchester College – one of the last and least likeable products of the Gothic Revival – in the 1890s. He himself specialised in a debased classical style easily recognisable by its mawkish mannerisms. Of this the Radcliffe Science Library (1933–4) and Trinity College's gateway to St Giles' (1947–8) are perhaps the most conspicuously displeasing examples: others are New College Library (1939), the Rose Lane Buildings of Merton College (1939–40), and the former History Faculty Library in Merton Street (built 1954–6 to designs made in 1938–9). Maufe (originally, as the college books testify, surnamed Muff) was a graduate of St. John's and his

183. Nuffield College: the tower as built in 1956.

177

principal works in Oxford were for his old college. They included the Dolphin Quadrangle at St. John's* (1947-8) and the Playhouse in Beaumont Street (1938). The latter is a model of architectural tact, while the former affirms with some success those conventional neo-Georgian virtues of solidity and proportion that Worthington went out of his way to deny. But if Maufe's architecture makes Worthington's look meretricious, it is sadly lacking in any virtues but those of a gentility unenlivened by wit, scholarship or spatial exploration (cf. fig. 173).

While Worthington and Maufe were busy in the colleges, a firm of architects called Lanchester and Lodge had a monopoly of work in the Science Area. Here, where there was no need to compromise with the past, something more enterprising might have been expected. But however well appointed within, the new laboratories built in the 1940s were, as architecture, totally contemptible. Built mostly of an anaemic beige brick, they aimed at a formality which was justified neither by their function nor by their siting, but failed utterly to achieve it. Here and there a pompous stone doorway with a coat of arms strikes an embarrassed attitude in the middle of a flat elevation full of large metal windows without architraves or adequate reveals. These buildings represent the final degeneration of a classical tradition of which Lanchester and Lodge were among the last incomprehending practitioners.

A particularly unfortunate characteristic of nearly all the Oxford architecture of this period (one from which only Maufe and Harrison were exempt) was the use, even for the most formal buildings, of rubble walling, apparently under the mistaken impression that Oxford colleges had some affinity with Cotswold barns and farm-houses, whereas in fact they had in the past invariably been built of properly dressed ashlar. Rubble walling had indeed been used by Jackson in some of his Jacobean Revival buildings, in much the same way as it was in some of the seventeenth-century manor-houses which constituted one of his major sources – that is to say for plain wall-surfaces, with plinths, quoins, etc., in dressed ashlar. In buildings of this kind (such as Jackson's additions to Trinity) the rubble is appropriately used and not at all prominent. But it was quite another matter when, at Rhodes House, Sir Herbert Baker, awkwardly marrying a miniature Pantheon to a Cotswold manor-house, clothed the former as well as the latter in the same rustic material, and Sir Giles Scott inexplicably followed suit in his New Bodleian Library (1937-40), a major public building in the heart of the city facing Hawksmoor's Clarendon Building. The result is like a dinner jacket made of Harris Tweed.

The man who did most to rouse Oxford from its architectural torpor was David Henderson, now Professor of Political Economy at University College, London, and then a Fellow of Lincoln College. Henderson's interest in architecture had been aroused by reading Sacheverell Sitwell's *British Architects and Craftsmen*. From Sitwell's evocation of past glories he moved on to the *Architectural Review*, then as now the intellectual man's guide to all that is most modern in architecture.

* An earlier design by J. J. Stevenson for a Gothic building on this site is preserved in the college archives.

178

No one who read the *Architectural Review* in the 1950s could doubt that Oxford dons were an architecturally retarded body, too much concerned to preserve and too little willing to create. In August 1952 the 'lack of aesthetic initiative' at Oxford and Cambridge was attacked by J.M. Richards in an article in which he reviewed recent building in both universities. Nuffield College, he said, represented a 'missed opportunity of a really tragic kind'. Maufe's work he found tolerable 'as period exercises go', but Worthington's (and Scott's) he denounced both for its 'whimsical eclecticism' and for its rubble stonework, 'utterly alien to the urbane dignity of Oxford with its fine tradition of ashlar masonry'. Everywhere he went he was appalled by 'the artistic barrenness and timidity of academic taste'. It was, he rightly said, 'the worst way of paying respect to ancient monuments to surround them with watered-down versions of themselves'. As for the Science Area, 'the total effect is more reminiscent of a modern trading estate than an ancient centre of learning'.

It was in the Science Area that David Henderson started the revolution that was soon to transform Oxford's architectural patronage. In 1955 he was elected Junior Proctor for the ensuing year, and as such a member of the Hebdomadal Council, the governing body of the University. Finding that yet another commission (for an extension to the Dyson Perrins (Organic Chemistry) Laboratory) was about to be given to Lanchester and Lodge, he succeeded in persuading Council to reconsider the choice of an architect. As Lanchester and Lodge's reign had been due as much to indifference as to any positive preference on the university's part, they were soon ousted in favour of architects suggested by Henderson. The Dyson Perrins extension (1957–9) and the Biochemistry Laboratory (1960–2) went to Basil Ward of Murray, Ward and Partners, the enlargement of the Pharmacology Department (1959–61) to Gollins, Melvin, Ward (E.F. Ward) and Partners. These, though buildings of no special distinction, were at least examples of modern building technology entirely appropriate to their respective functions. Basil Ward, a masterly manager of committees, was soon as firmly established in the continually expanding Science Area as Lanchester and Lodge had been a decade earlier. When, in 1956, he was invited to plan the 'Keble Triangle', an area newly appropriated to scientific purposes, Henderson (who had by then completed his term of office as Proctor) felt that this important commission ought to have been made the subject of an open competition, and moved a motion to that effect in Congregation. Although he was outmanœuvred by Ward (who succeeded in warning off the intended assessors of the competition), Henderson's motion was not without its effect: it aroused 'a general discontent within the University both about Oxford architecture in recent decades and about . . . future planning policy'. Ward remained in control of the Keble Triangle, where in due course he designed and built the obtrusive and crudely detailed Engineering Laboratory (1960). But a 'Committee on elevations and the choice of architects' was established which for the next twenty years ensured that the University's architectural patronage was exercised in a more enlightened manner.

Meanwhile Henderson had directly or indirectly been instrumental in recommending some of the best contemporary architects to colleagues in other colleges where building was in contemplation. A visit to Denmark led him to mention the name of Arne Jacobsen at a time when another completely new college, St. Catherine's, was being planned, and at Corpus (1957) he suggested the Architects' Co-Partnership when Maufe's proposals for remodelling the President's Lodgings there proved to be unsatisfactory.

The remodelling of the Corpus Lodgings was in fact the first work in an Oxford college to be carried out to the design of an architect not committed to the kind of exhausted historicism represented by Worthington and Maufe. But it presented only one small elevation to the world. The architects wanted this to be faced with brick, but the Local Authority refused, so the Co-Partnership had ashlar cut up and laid in narrow courses like brickwork. The result, though indubitably 'modern', and not unpleasing, was too idiosyncratic to be seen as a decisive victory for a new architectural style.

The first major college building designed in an uncompromisingly modern style was the 'Beehive' in the North Quadrangle at St. John's (1958–60). Here again the Architects' Co-Partnership in the person of Michael Powers were superseding Sir Edward Maufe and superseding him on his own ground, for Maufe was not merely a graduate of the college, but an Honorary Fellow as well. His long connection with St. John's, the esteem in which he was held by the senior fellows, and his eminence in his profession, made it difficult to dethrone him. But it was imperative to do so if the North Quadrangle was to be completed in an architecturally satisfactory manner. The formation of this quadrangle had been a long-drawn out process, going back to a design made in 1880 by George Gilbert Scott junior (fig. 184, A). Of this only the western (street) front had been erected between 1880 and 1900. Complete with entrance-tower and gateway, it may be criticised for looking too much like a second college and too little like the extension of an existing one. Nevertheless it is a handsome building whose bold gargoyles and other embellishments successfully recapture the Gothic spirit.* The north side of the quadrangle was built to a different, but still fairly convincing, sub-Gothic design by N.W. Harrison in 1909 (fig. 184, B). But in the north–east corner, added by Maufe in 1933, the elevations are further simplified into a vestigial Gothic that is all but lifeless. To complete the quadrangle Maufe proposed to add three more identical staircases (fig. 184, C). What is more he proposed to do so on an alignment which would impinge on the Senior Common Room at an obtuse angle. The result would have been a broken-backed quadrangle as well as one in which the last senility of the Gothic Revival would be for ever manifest.

In Maufe's defeat at St. John's David Henderson played no part. It was an internal revolution independently instigated by some of the junior fellows of the college with the help and advice (as to possible architects) of Sir John Summerson.

* Scott at first proposed the rather indecisive mixture of Gothic and Jacobean detailing seen in fig. 185, but the college insisted that the building should have a 'medieval' rather than a 'renaissance' character. Scott's scheme included a new hall, for which he made the Jacobean design seen in fig. 186. This, of course, was not built in any form.

180

184. (*facing page*) St. John's College: the development of the North Quadrangle, showing the schemes proposed in 1880 and 1956 and the buildings subsequently erected (based on plans in St. John's College muniments).

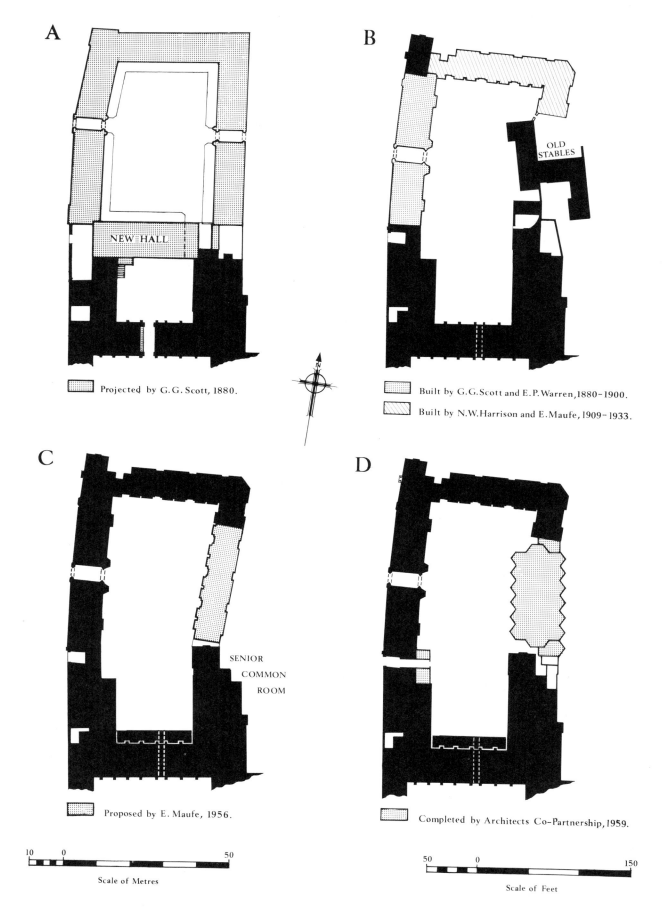

A

Projected by G.G. Scott, 1880.

B

OLD STABLES

Built by G.G. Scott and E.P. Warren, 1880–1900.

Built by N.W. Harrison and E. Maufe, 1909–1933.

NEW HALL

C

SENIOR COMMON ROOM

Proposed by E. Maufe, 1956.

D

Completed by Architects Co-Partnership, 1959.

10   0   50

Scale of Metres

50   0   150

Scale of Feet

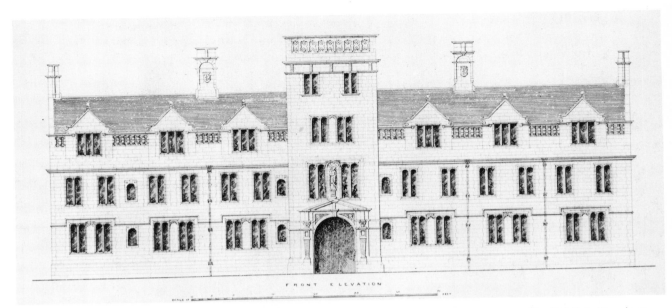

FRONT ELEVATION

SCALE OF

185. St. John's College: first design for the St. Giles' front of the North Quadrangle, by G. G. Scott, 1880 (R.I.B.A. Drawings Collection).

186. St. John's College: G. G. Scott's design for the new hall shown on plan in figure 184 A (R.I.B.A. Drawings Collection).

182

The cellular plan, made up of hexagonal rooms, reflected an interest in organic form current among architects at the time: but here (besides giving every room a southern aspect) it produced a broken outline which was sympathetic to the projections and recessions of Scott's building opposite, and enabled the awkward alignment of the east side of the quadrangle to be rectified in a neat and unobtrusive manner (fig. 184, D).

By 1960 the battle for modern architecture in Oxford had been won. By 1977, when Lord Bullock (the Master of St. Catherine's College) contributed a foreword to an illustrated review of *New Architecture* in Oxford, 'the change in attitude and the recovery of nerve' had, as he observed, been such that Oxford and Cambridge offered to the visitor one of the best and most representative collections of British architecture during the previous twenty years. The 1960s and 1970s proved, in fact, to be for Oxford another of those periods of intensive building activity that have characterised her architectural history. The incentive in this case was an increasing population both of graduates and of undergraduates at a time when the traditional lodging-house was in decline. To this some colleges were able to respond by the conversion of existing houses, but for others a new building was often the only possible solution. Not everything built during these years can be commended. To say that Magdalen's Waynflete Building (1960–1) is unworthy of its magnificent site is to understate a major architectural tragedy. New College's Sacher Building (1961–2) fails lamentably to accommodate itself to the modest street of vernacular houses into which it thrusts its self-assertive bulk. As for Queen's Florey Building (1971) it demonstrates all too well Le Corbusier's inhumane concept of a domestic building as a habitable machine. But the elegant precision of Arne Jacobsen's St. Catherine's, the expressive anatomy of Philip Dowson's additions to Somerville and St. John's, and the bold buttress-like forms of Powell and Moya's Blue Boar Quadrangle at Christ Church, even Ahrends, Burton and Koralek's disconcerting combination, at Keble, of glass curtain-walling with brick carapace – all these are admirable in their several ways, and a vindication of those who in the late 1950s strove to make Oxford a place where architecture was once more a living art and not just an antiquarian exercise.

In a period as architecturally active as the 1960s and 1970s it naturally happened that many alternative schemes were considered and rejected. Several grand designs, notably those of Howell, Killick, Partridge and Amis for St. Anne's College (fig. 187) and of Sir Leslie Martin for Wellington Square, were only partially realised, and almost every executed building has left its legacy of modified or rejected plans. At least two limited competitions were held (for the Sir Thomas White Quadrangle at St. John's in 1967, and for internal reconstruction at Magdalen in 1975), and college bursaries are full of dusty models and rolls of half-forgotten drawings. To attempt to disinter all these schemes would be tedious and in some cases impolitic. Moreover it would tend to overbalance this book with the architectural casualties of the recent past. Two only of the most spectacular must be allowed to conclude this chapter: the Zoology Tower (1962) and the Pitt-Rivers Museum (1967).

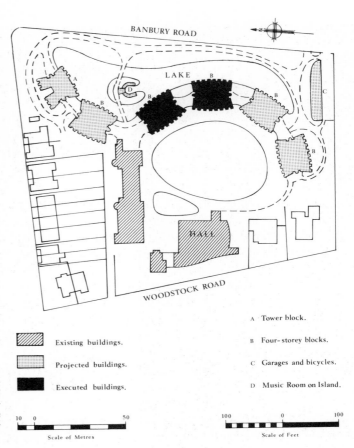

BANBURY ROAD

LAKE

WOODSTOCK ROAD

187. St. Anne's College: plan for
new buildings round a lake proposed by Howell, Killick, Partridge
and Amis in 1961 (redrawn by
Daphne Hart).

Existing buildings.

Projected buildings.

Executed buildings.

A   Tower block.

B   Four-storey blocks.

C   Garages and bicycles.

D   Music Room on Island.

10   0   50

Scale of Metres

100   0   100

Scale of Feet

The scheme for the Zoology Tower followed the appointment in 1961 of J. W. S.
Pringle as Professor of Zoology. The existing Department of Zoology was quite
inadequate for the needs of a rapidly developing subject, and at the time of his
appointment the new professor was given assurances that a suitable building
would be provided. This proved to be impossible in the already overcrowded
Science Area, and the solution recommended by the architects (Chamberlin,
Powell and Bon) was a twenty-five storey tower sited in the University Parks just
outside the existing boundary of the Science Area. They argued that the relationship between the Parks and the Science Area should be one of inter-penetration
rather than of rigid and 'occlusive' separation, and that slim tower, some two
hundred and sixty feet high but only fifty feet square, would not be detrimental
either to Oxford as a whole or to the Parks in particular. But although its profile
was broken up by alternate projection and recession (fig. 188), the proposed tower
was hardly elegant in appearance, and the building that the Vice-Chancellor
optimistically described as likely to bring 'a touch of San Gimignano' into the
Oxford skyline, seemed to others 'less like San Gimignano set down in the Science
Area than like the new Engineering Laboratory set down in San Gimignano'. In
any case any further encroachment on the Parks was calculated to arouse general
hostility, whatever the merits of the building itself. In June 1962 Congregation

184

188. The Zoology Tower whose construction in the University Parks was proposed in 1962, a photograph of a model (Messrs. Chamberlin, Powell and Bon).

185

189. The Pitt-Rivers Museum: photograph of a model exhibited in 1968 (from the prospectus of 1969).

rejected the scheme by a large majority, and (following a comprehensive review of the needs of the science departments by Sir William Holford) a more acceptable solution was found in the form of a monumental but much less obtrusive building designed by Sir Leslie Martin and built on a site in Merton Playing Fields.

The Zoology Tower was regretted by few. But the failure to build the new Pitt-Rivers Museum designed by Pier Luigi Nervi in collaboration with Powell and Moya has deprived Oxford of a spectacular architectural concept which would have delighted many besides anthropologists. Although the architecture was to be Nervi's, the concept was due to Bernard Fagg, the Museum's curator. For many years the collections in his care had demanded more space and a better form of display. General Pitt-Rivers had been one of the pioneers of typological study both in archaeology and in anthropology, and when he gave his collections to the University in 1884 it was on the understanding that they would be arranged on a typological basis. For students of art or of some particular artefact, this is ideal, but it is less so for those whose interest is primarily in a specific society or a single geographical area. As early as 1963 Fagg had worked out a method of reconciling

186

typology with geography. The exhibits would be arranged in concentric circles, each of which would represent one typological sequence, while each segment of the circular gallery would be devoted to a specific culture or area. The typological visitor would follow a circular path, the geographical one a radial one. In the middle there would be a tropical and sub-tropical plant house, with localised humidity control, to present the natural background appropriate to the adjoining cultures. It was an elegant and imaginative solution to a unique problem in museum arrangement, but it demanded a very large circular area all on one floor and a correspondingly extensive roof. A dome was the obvious answer, and Nervi the man to design it. His drawings, dated 1967, show a rotunda of fenestrated concrete rising in the middle of the circular galleries (fig. 189). By sinking the two lowest floors the height of the main structure could be kept down to thirty-five feet – an important consideration if the building were to be built (as was the intention) on a site off the Banbury Road in the residential area of North Oxford.

The structural problem was well within the capacity of the reinforced concrete technology of which Nervi was a master, and the complex patterns of the ceilings, culminating in the dome, would have had something of the quality of a great Gothic vault (fig. 190). The project was, perhaps, the last chance for the university to build in the twentieth century something that would take its place with the Divinity School, the Radcliffe Library and the Ashmolean Museum as a major work of European architecture. Only money to build it (about £3,000,000 was the estimate in 1968) was lacking, and in the end, despite general admiration for the design, it was the failure to find an opportune benefactor that brought the whole scheme to naught.

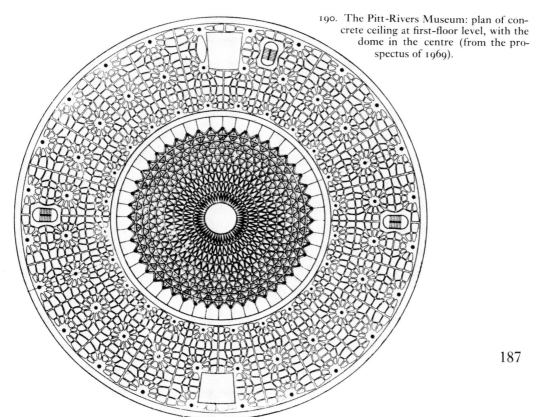

190. The Pitt-Rivers Museum: plan of concrete ceiling at first-floor level, with the dome in the centre (from the prospectus of 1969).

187

Sources and Bibliography

E.H. Cordeaux & D.H. Merry, *A Bibliography of Printed Works relating to the University of Oxford* (1968)

E.H. Cordeaux & D.H. Merry, *A Bibliography of Printed Works relating to the City of Oxford* (Oxford Historical Society N.S. xxv, 1976)

Victoria County History, *Oxfordshire*, vol. iii, *The University of Oxford*, ed. M.D. Lobel (1954), vol. iv, *The City of Oxford*, ed. A. Crossley (1979)

Royal Commission on Historical Monuments: *City of Oxford* (1939)

Nikolaus Pevsner, 'Oxford' in Sherwood & Pevsner, *Oxfordshire* (the Buildings of England, 1974)

David Loggan, *Oxonia Illustrata* (1675)

James Ingram, *Memorials of Oxford*, 3 vols. (1837)

H.M. Colvin, *A Biographical Dictionary of British Architects 1600–1840* (1978)

I. Gothic Uncertainties

T.G. Hassall, 'Excavations at Oxford', *Oxoniensia*, xxxiv–xxxix (1969–74)

T.G. Hassall, *Oxford, the city beneath your feet: archaeological excavations in the City of Oxford 1967–1972* (1972)

G. Lambrick & H. Woods, 'Excavations on the Second Site of the Dominican Priory, Oxford', *Oxoniensia*, xli (1976)

Epistolae Academicae Oxon., ed. H. Anstey, i (Oxford Historical Society, 1898), p. 192 (contract with Thomas Elkyn, mason, 1440)

F.E. Howard, 'Richard Winchcombe's work at the Divinity School and elsewhere' in *Adderbury Rectoria*, ed. T.F. Hobson (Oxfordshire Record Society, 1926), pp. 34–41.

A. Vallance, *The Old Colleges of Oxford* (1912)

New College Oxford 1379–1979, ed. J. Buxton & P. Williams (1979), 'The Building of the Medieval College', by Gervase Jackson-Stops

H.M. Colvin, 'The Building of St. Bernard's College', *Oxoniensia*, xxiv (1959)

J.G. Milne & J.H. Harvey, 'The Building of Cardinal College', *Oxoniensia*, viii–ix (1943–4)

Bodleian Library, Twyne MS. 21, pp. 350-7 (building account of Cardinal College)

Letters and Papers of Henry VIII, ed. Brewer, iv(2), no. 2734 (letter from Dr. John London describing works at Cardinal College, 29 Dec. 1526)

F. Haverfield, note on the architecture of Christ Church in *Proceedings of the Society of Antiquaries*, 2nd. series, xxii (1909), pp. 424-30

II. Retarded Renaissance

I.G. Philip, 'The building of the Schools Quadrangle', *Oxoniensia*, xiii (1948)

Letters of Sir Thomas Bodley to Thomas James, ed. G.W. Wheeler (1926), pp. xxxviii-xxxix, 223

John Newman, 'Oxford libraries before 1800', *Archaeological Journal*, vol. 135 (1978), pp. 248-57

Anon., 'The Arts End of the Bodleian Library', *Oxford Magazine*, 28 Oct. 1937, pp. 86-7

Lucy Gent, *Picture and Poetry 1560-1620* (1981), p. 75 (on Oxford book-lists 1550-1650)

Q. Skinner, *Foundations of Modern Political Thought*, i (1978), pp. 94-101 (for the concepts of *Virtus* and Honour exemplified at Caius College, Cambridge)

University College archives: pasteboard model and unexecuted plan, *c.* 1634

III. The Limits of a Private Purse

C. Wren, *Parentalia* (1750), p. 335

John Summerson, *The Sheldonian in its Time: an oration delivered to commemorate the restoration of the Theatre 16 November 1963* (1964)

The Correspondence of Henry Oldenburg, ed. A.R. & M. Hall, ii (1966), pp. 44-5

Familiar Letters, ed. F. Astle (1767), p. 110 (letter of Abraham Hill, 1663)

The Life and Times of Anthony Wood, ed. A. Clark, iv (Oxford Historical Society, 1895), pp. 71-2

Wren Society, xix (1942), pp. 91-9 (Sheldonian Theatre)

John Orrell, 'Inigo Jones at the Cockpit', *Shakespeare Survey*, xxx (1977)

Trinity College archives, Miscellanea, vol. 1

New College Oxford 1379-1979, ed. J. Buxton & P. Williams (1979), 'Gains and Losses: the College Buildings, 1404-1750', by Gervase Jackson-Stops

IV. Dr. Clarke's Portfolios

C. Owen, *Carmen Pindaricum in Theatrum Sheldonianum ... recitatum Julii die 9⁰ anno 1669* (1669)

W.G. Hiscock, *Henry Aldrich* (1960)

H.M. Colvin, 'The Architects of All Saints Church, Oxford', *Oxoniensia*, xix (1954)

The Journeys of Celia Fiennes, ed. C. Morris (1949), p. 36

H.M. Petter, *The Oxford Almanacks* (1974)

H.M. Colvin, *Catalogue of Architectural Drawings of the Eighteenth and Nineteenth Centuries in the Library of Worcester College, Oxford* (1964)

Kerry Downes, *Hawksmoor* (1959)

Historical MSS. Commission, *Portland*, vii (1901), p. 217 (letter of Dr. W. Stratford to Harley, 20 Sept. 1716)

W. Williams, *Oxonia Depicta* (1732-3)

V. Hawksmoor's Oxford

H.M. Colvin, *Catalogue of Architectural Drawings of the Eighteenth and Nineteenth Centuries in the Library of Worcester College, Oxford* (1964)

Kerry Downes, *Hawksmoor* (1959)

The Building Accounts of the Radcliffe Camera, ed. S.G. Gillam (Oxford Historical Society, N.S. xiii, 1958)

S. Lang, 'Cambridge and Oxford Reformed: Hawksmoor as Town Planner', *Architectural Review*, vol. 103, April 1948

S. Lang, 'By Hawksmoor out of Gibbs' (the Radcliffe Camera), *Architectural Review*, vol. 105, April 1949

James Gibbs, *Bibliotheca Radcliviana: or, A short account of the Radcliffe Library* (1747)

H. Hager, 'Carlo Fontana and the Jesuit Sanctuary at Loyola', *Journal of the Warburg & Courtauld Institutes*, xxxvii (1974)

Bodleian Library, minute-books and accounts of the Radcliffe Trustees

VI. Indecision at Magdalen

Magdalen College Library: architectural drawings in bound volumes and portfolios; MS 732: 'Architectural Changes at Magdalen College' by J.R. Bloxam

Magdalen College Archives:

Benefactors' Book

Order Books

Correspondence, accounts and plans relating to the New Buildings, *c.* 1720-40

New Building Account (CP 2/51)

Reports by Bodley & Garner, Champneys, Street and Wilkinson on designs submitted in competition, 1879

Notes on plans submitted by architects, 1879 (220/32)

The Magdalen College Register, ed. J.R. Bloxam, 7 vols. 1853-85; new series ed. W.D. Macray, 8 vols. 1894-1911

T.S.R. Boase, 'An Oxford College and the Gothic Revival', *Journal of the Warburg & Courtauld Institutes*, xviii (1955)

[J.C. Buckler], *Observations on the original architecture of Saint Mary Magdalen College, Oxford; and on the innovations anciently or recently attempted* (1823)

Kerry Downes, *Hawksmoor* (1959), pp. 154-5
R.D. Middleton, *Magdalen Studies* (1936), chap. 2 (on J.R. Bloxam)
R.D. Middleton, *Dr. Routh* (1938)
Country Life, 30 May 1947, p. 1017 (design for building by Oliver Hill)

VII. Pugin and the Battle for Balliol

Balliol College Library: architectural drawings by Wyatt, Basevi and Pugin
John Bryson, 'The Balliol that might have been: Pugin's rejected design', *Country Life*, 27 June 1963
John Jones, 'The Civil War of 1843', *Balliol College Record* (1978)
Michael Trappes-Lomax, *Pugin* (1933), pp. 138-40
Oxford Chronicle, 11 Jan. 1845
Wilfrid Ward, *William George Ward and the Oxford Movement* (1890), pp. 154-5
Andrew Saint & Michael Kaser, *St. Antony's College, Oxford: A History of its Buildings and Site* (1973)

VIII. The Two Museums

Cambridge Competitions:
  David Watkin, *The Triumph of the Classical: Cambridge Architecture 1804-1834* (Fitzwilliam Museum, Cambridge, 1977)
St. Martin's Church, Carfax, Oxford:
  Parish Records in Bodleian Library, including papers and minutes of the Building Committee (MSS. d.d. Par. Oxon. St. Martin's)
  C.J.H. Fletcher, *A History of the Church and Parish of St. Martin, Oxford* (1896)
  Wyatt Papworth, *John B. Papworth* (privately printed 1879), pp. 119-21
  MS. Diary of Thomas Rickman in British Architectural Library, R.I.B.A., London
  Drawings by J.B. Papworth in R.I.B.A. Drawings Collection, London
The Shire Hall, Oxford:
  Oxfordshire County Record Office, Courts of Justice Committee Minute Book, 1836-41 (QSC VII/1)
  Bodleian Library, G.A. fol. A.139: *Suggestions to Architects or Builders who intend to offer Plans and Estimates for a Shire Hall and Courts of Justice for the County of Oxford*, 1837
  Oxford Journal, 14 Jan. and 8 April 1837
The Martyrs' Memorial:
  J.P. Wells, 'The Martyrs' Memorial', *Oxford Magazine*, 2 Feb. 1968
  Bodleian Library, MS. Top. Oxon b. 112 (papers relating to the Memorial); MS. Top. Gen. a.4, f.8 (design by J.M. Derick); University Archives NW 15/16 (printed *Information and Instructions to the Architects who have been invited to favour the Committee with Designs for the Memorial Cross*)
  G.G. Scott, *Personal and Professional Recollections* (1879), pp. 89-90

The Ashmolean Museum:
  Bodleian Library: University Archives, minutes, etc. of the Delegates for the
    Taylor and Randolph Building (TLF/18/1, TLM/1/1); MS. Top. Oxon. c.
    202 (various papers, including list of competitors); MS. Top. Oxon. a.9
    (design by G. Gutch and E.W. Trendall); MS. Top. Oxon. b. 89 (drawing
    of hemicycle)
  Builder, iv (1846), pp. 510-11
  David Watkin, *The Life and Work of C.R. Cockerell* (1974), chap. xii
  The Oxford University, City & County Herald, 10 June 1841 (illustration of
    Cockerell's first design)
The University Museum:
  Oxford University Archives
    UM/M/1/1, Minutes of the Delegates for the University Museum, 1853-8
    UM/P/3/1-7, Contract drawings dated 1855
    NW 2/1, Papers relating to the University Museum, 1853-4
  Bodleian Library, G.A. Oxon. c.70 (244-6) and c.75 (287), flysheets concerning
    the University Museum
  R. Greswell, *Memorial on the (proposed) Oxford University Lecture Rooms,
    Library, Museums etc., addressed to Congregation* (May 1853)
  G.E. Street, *A Plea for the Revival of True Principles of Architecture in the
    Public Buildings of Oxford* (1853), also printed in the *Builder*, xi (1853), pp.
    403-4
  [J.H. Parker], *The Old English Style of Architecture as applicable to Modern
    Requirements, or Suggestions for the New Museum at Oxford* [1853]
  H.M. & K.D. Vernon, *A History of the Oxford Museum* (1909)
  H.W. Acland & John Ruskin, *The Oxford Museum* (1859, enlarged ed. 1893)
  A. Vernon Harcourt, *The Oxford Museum and its Founders*, reprinted from the
    Cornhill Magazine for March 1910
  Builder, xii (1854), pp. 590-1, 657; xiii (1855), pp. 291-2, 318-9; xvii (1859),
    p. 401.
  F. O'Dwyer & Jeremy Williams, 'Benjamin Woodward', in *Victorian Dublin*,
    ed. T. Kennedy (1980)
  James Fergusson, *History of the Modern Styles of Architecture* (1862), pp.
    327-8

IX. Jackson and the Jacobean Revival

Recollections of Thomas Graham Jackson, ed. B.H. Jackson (1950)
C.E. Mallows, 'The Complete Works of T.G. Jackson', *Architectural Review*, i
  (1897), pp. 136-60
Christ Church Belfry:
  Christ Church archives: minutes of the Governing Body, 1874; minutes of the
    Belfry Committee (xlix a.1); architectural drawings by Jackson and Bodley
    & Garner

Architect, 18 Sept. 1875

Builder, 7 Nov. 1874, p. 933

Building News, 27 June 1879, p. 720

C.L. Dodgson, *The New Belfry of Christ Church, Oxford* by D.C.L. (1872), *The Vision of the Three Ts*, by the Author of 'The New Belfry' (1873)

Bodleian Library, design for belfry by Sir Gilbert Scott (Dep. a.17/4)

The Examination Schools:

Bodleian Library: University Archives, Minutes of the Delegates for building the Examination Schools, 1875–89; G.A. Oxon. c. 33, Basil Champneys' and T.G. Jackson's descriptions of their designs; G.A. Oxon. 8° 164 (9), Bodley & Garner's description of their design; pamphlets, flysheets, etc., in G.A. Oxon. 4° 119 (2), G.A. Oxon. b. 138, f. 86 and G.A. Oxon. 8° 161 (21); MS. Top. Oxon. a. 43–44 (R), designs by J.O. Scott, 1876; MS. Top. Oxon. a.19, designs and working drawings by T.G. Jackson

Oxford University Gazette, i (1870), 22 March, 15 Nov., 6 Dec.; iv (1873), pp. 153–4 (supplement), 168, 191; v (1875), pp. 499, 552, 593, 644; vi (1876), pp. 406–9 (Jackson's description of his design), 441–2

H.H.E. Craster, *History of the Bodleian Library* (1952)

Architect, ix (1873), pp. 246, 291; x (1873), p. 57 (illustration of Deane's design); xxvii (1882), pp. 362–3

Builder, xlii (1882), pp. 719–20

Building News, xxix (1875), 1 Oct. (illustration of J.O. Scott's design); xxx (1876), 28 April (J.O. Scott's design); xxxi (1876), 1 Sept. (J.O. Scott's design), 8 Sept. (J.O. Scott's entrance hall), 17 Nov. (Champneys' design), 22 Dec. (Jackson's design); xxxvi (1879), 27 June (Jackson's entrance hall)

The High School for Boys:

Oxford City Archives: Governors' Minute Book, 1878–1910

Bodleian Library, G.A. Oxon. c. 111 (printed statement, 1877)

Building News, 13, 20 Feb., 19 March 1880, pp. 190, 237, 340

The High School for Girls:

Oxford High School, Girls Public Day School Trust, 1875–1960, ed. V.E. Stack (Abingdon, 1963), pp. 3–4

Brasenose College:

T.G. Jackson, 'The High Street of Oxford and Brasenose College', *Magazine of Art*, August 1889, pp. 332–40

E.W. Allfrey, *The Architectural History of the College*, Brasenose College Quatercentenary Monographs no. iii (1909), pp. 46–62

The Town Hall:

Oxford City Archives: Council Minutes 1889–92, pp. 326–7, 347; Report of the General Purposes Committee 29 June 1892; printed description of designs nos. 11, 16, 32, 45, 48, 57

Bodleian Library, G.A. Oxon. c. 107 (14): *Instructions to Architects engaged in the first competition*, 1891

Architect, vol. 47

Builder, 10 Nov. 1892 (design by Halsey Ricardo); 10 Dec. 1892 (design by Thomas Davison)

Building News, 1 Jan.; 24 June; 1 July 1892 (account of competition); 8 July 1892 (designs by J.B. Hipkins, Charles Bell, Perkin & Cheston, H.T. Hare); 15 July (design by Ernest Runtz); 22 July (design by Charles Bell); 29 July (design by Perkin & Cheston)

X. *Oxford and the Modern Movement*

G.V. Cox, *Recollections of Oxford* (1870), pp. 404-5

David Watkin, *Morality and Architecture* (1977), part I

W.A. Pantin, 'The Oxford Architectural and Historical Society, 1839-1939', *Oxoniensia*, iv (1939)

Oxford University Archives, AM/11 (proposed Professorship of the History of Architecture, 1946)

St. John's College Muniments, Belbroughton Road leases

Balliol College Library, architectural designs by Samuel & Harding, 1936

All Souls College archives: minutes of the Governing Body 1930-9 (extracts kindly provided by Mr. J.S.G. Simmons); minutes of the building committee, 1946-53; architectural drawings by A.S.G. Butler (1930), W.G. Newton (1938), Maxwell Fry (1938), Scott, Shepherd & Breakwell (1938) and C.H. James (1946)

Architect, 16 May 1947, p 131 (illustration of C.H. James's design for All Souls)

Maxwell Fry, *Autobiographical Sketches* (1975) , pp. 153-4

R.I.B.A. Drawings Collection, London, architectural design for All Souls by E. Maufe (1951)

Oxford University Archives: printed *Proceedings of the Nuffield College Committee* (M27^b); Minutes of the Nuffield College Committee (UDC/M27^a/1); file of the architectural sub-committee (NH/4B/1-3)

Royal Institute of British Architects, London: application of A. St. B. Harrison for admission as a Fellow of the Institute, 1927

The Times, 14 Feb. 1976, obituary of A. St. B. Harrison

Lawrence Durrell, *Bitter Lemons* (1957)

Nuffield College Library: architectural drawings by Harrison, Barnes & Hubbard

Oxford Magazine, 8 June 1939, p. 707, verses on the New Bodleian Library by 'Judson' (Neville Coghill)

J.M. Richards, 'Recent Building in Oxford and Cambridge', *Architectural Review*, vol. 112, August 1952, pp. 73-9

Oxford Magazine, 18 Oct. 1956, pp. 20-1; 15 Nov. 1956, p. 116; 22 Nov. 1956, p. 126; 6 Dec. 1956, p. 186 (Keble Road triangle)

Corpus Christi College, Oxford: The President's Lodgings (printed for the College, 1959)

St. John's College Muniments: architectural drawings by G.G. Scott, junior, J.J. Stevenson, E.P. Warren, N.W. Harrison, Sir Edward Maufe and the

Architects' Co-Partnership

R.I.B.A. Drawings Catalogue, *The Scott Family*, ed. Joanna Heseltine (1981), p. 151

ed. David Smith & Godfrey Marks, *New Oxford, a guide to the modern city* (O.U. Design Society, 1961)

David Reed & Philip Opher, *New Architecture in Oxford* (Oxford Polytechnic, 1977)

The Architects' Journal, 20 April 1961, pp. 565–6 (scheme for St. Anne's College by Howell, Killick, Partridge & Amis); 20 June 1961, p. 1362 (design for Zoology Tower by Chamberlin, Powell & Bon)

Oxford Magazine, 23 Nov. 1961; 22 Feb. 1962; 21 June 1962 (Zoology Tower)

Oxford University Gazette, 21 June, 6 Dec. 1962 (Zoology Tower)

The New Pitt-Rivers Museum and proposed Centre for the study of Anthropology and Human Environment (prospectus, 1969)

Index